YOUNT V. MOLITOR

Trial Materials

YOUNT V. MOLITOR

Trial Materials

Paul J. Zwier
Emory University School of Law

William J. Hunt
Clark, Hunt, Ahern & Embry

NITA
NATIONAL INSTITUTE FOR TRIAL ADVOCACY

Address inquiries to:
Reprint Permission
National Institute for Trial Advocacy
1685 38th Street, Suite 200
Boulder, CO 80301-2735
Phone: (800) 225-6482
Fax: (720) 890-7069
Email: permissions@nita.org

ISBN 978-1-60156-542-6
eISBN 978-1-60156-543-3

FBA 1542

Printed in the United States of America

Wolters Kluwer

Official co-publisher of NITA.
WKLegaledu.com/NITA

Contents

INTRODUCTION

The plaintiff, Stephen (Fred) Yount, has brought an action for breach of contract against his former employer and business partner, Harold Molitor.

Yount majored in business in college. He was a recent graduate when he started with Molitor, and he worked his entire career (fifteen years) with Molitor until they parted ways.

Molitor, born YR-59, is significantly older than Yount, and he considered Yount to be his protégé. When Yount started with Molitor, Molitor was running a small factory. Molitor later bought and sold similar factories and then moved on to running what became, in essence, a *boiler room*,[1] buying and selling mostly shares of penny stocks in companies that generally went out of business. Yount helped Molitor in all his business ventures through the years and became Molitor's right-hand man. Molitor came to consider Yount almost as a son. Molitor made his money on transaction costs and selling shares. He also operated a limited partnership known as the Molitor Technology Fund, an entity in which the limited partners would contribute sums of money for the partnership shares and the limited partnership, in turn, would buy shares of lightly traded and/or restricted stock through Molitor. Molitor also was compensated as the general partner and manager of the fund.

Regulators had opened more than one investigation into Molitor Technology Fund business. Yount was simply someone who worked there and was never, to his knowledge, investigated.

In early YR-6, the stock market made a sudden downturn after a tech bubble had burst. Demand for stock in start-up companies evaporated. In addition, the Molitor Technology Fund business started to unravel. Yount decided it was time for him to leave.

When Yount told Molitor that he was leaving, he claimed that Molitor owed him $7,212 in expenses. In lieu of payment of the expenses, Molitor alleges that he and Yount reached an agreement that Yount would be entitled to certain securities that would be delivered to Yount by May 31, YR-5. The list of these securities is contained in the expert's report.

1 In business, the term "boiler room" refers to an outbound call center selling questionable investments by telephone. It typically refers to a room where salesmen use unfair, dishonest sales tactics, sometimes selling penny stock, private placements, or committing outright stock fraud. The term carries a negative connotation, and it is often used to imply high-pressure sales tactics and, sometimes, poor working conditions. A boiler room usually has an undisclosed relationship with the company being promoted or undisclosed profit from the sale of the house stock they are promoting. The managers of the boiler room usually have close ties to the same owners of the company whose stock is being promoted. After the sales force of the boiler room sells their clients on the idea of the initial public offering (IPO), they are not allowed to sell the shares that the customer invested. This is because there is no real "market" for the shares, so any shares sold before buyers are attracted would create a large loss in the price of the stock because it is being thinly traded with no public support. Once the insider investors are in place, a boiler room promotes (via telephone calls to brokerage clients or spam email) these thinly traded stocks where there is no actual market. The brokers of the boiler room actually "create" a market by attracting buyers, whose demand for the stock drives up the price. This gives the owners of the company enough volume to sell their shares at a profit, a form of pump-and-dump operation where the original investors profit at the expense of the investors taken in by the boiler-room operation.

The securities were never delivered, and on October 6, YR-4, an amended severance agreement was signed by Yount and Molitor, requiring delivery by January 31, YR-3. The securities were not delivered on January 31, YR-3, and Yount sued. The suit was brought in YR-2.

Most of stock listed in the agreement was worthless. However, two stocks are claimed to have had value during the time the agreement was specified. The first is TelexGlobal, and it is the main reason for the lawsuit. Yount claims that the value of the TelexGlobal stock on January 31, YR-3, was $208,832.63, based on the report of his expert. In addition, Yount claims value from a stock called Nevada Software Technology Applications Inc., otherwise known as Standard TECH. Yount claims this stock was worth $156,250.00, also according to his expert.

The defendant, Molitor, denies that he ever had a contract to deliver the listed stock, any intended delivery was meant as a gift, and Yount's claims failed for want of delivery and for want of consideration. In addition, even if such a contract existed, each of the listed stocks was restricted stock (Rule 144 required a one-year holding period), and it would have been unlikely that Yount would have been able to remove the restrictions in time to claim the value in these stocks before they lost any value they might have had. TelexGlobal was valueless within one year of January 31, YR-3.

Electronic exhibits can be found at the following website:

http://bit.ly/1P20Jea
Password: YountTrial1

Stipulations

1. Exhibit 12 is a learned treatise and will be treated as such by the trial judge.
2. All years in these materials are stated in the following form:

   YR-0 indicates the actual year in which the case is being tried (i.e., the present year);

   YR-1 indicates the preceding year (please use the actual year);

   YR-2 indicates the next preceding year (please use the actual year); et cetera.

ACKNOWLEDGMENT

The National Institute for Trial Advocacy wishes to thank Facebook for its permission to use likenesses of its website as part of these teaching materials.

STATE OF NITA

CENTRAL, ss.	**SUPERIOR COURT** **CIVIL ACTION NO.**
STEPHEN F. YOUNT, **Plaintiff** **v.** **MOLITOR MANAGEMENT GROUP, INC., and HAROLD A. MOLITOR** **Defendants**	**COMPLAINT**

PARTIES

1. The plaintiff in this matter is Stephen F. Yount, an individual who resides at 204 Seaview Court, Nita City, Nita 01532.

2. A defendant in this case is Molitor Management Group, Inc., a Nita corporation with offices located at 24 Yardley Executive Park, Yardley, Nita 01533.

3. A defendant in this case is Harold A. Molitor, an individual who resides at 55 Marbleridge Road, Topsfield, Nita 01845.

STATEMENT OF THE CASE

4. As recently as YR-4, the plaintiff, Stephen F. Yount, was an employee of Molitor Management Group, Inc.

5. At all times relevant hereto, Harold A. Molitor was the Chairman of Molitor Management Group, Inc.

6. On or about April 30, YR-5, an agreement entitled Severance Agreement (the Agreement) was entered into by and between Stephen F. Yount, Molitor Management Group, Inc., and Harold A. Molitor, individually.

7. The Agreement provided, in relevant part, that "(i)n lieu of $7,212.00 owed to Stephen F. Yount (SFY) by Molitor Management Group, Inc. (MMG), SFY will purchase from MMG and Harold A. Molitor for said amount the following interests." The Agreement listed certain securities that were subject to the purchase. A true and complete copy of the Severance Agreement is attached hereto as Exhibit 1 and incorporated by reference.

8. The Agreement further provided, after the list of securities, in relevant part, that "Harold Molitor will cause those interests above currently in his or MMG's possession to be transferred to SFY by May 31, YR-4, with the remainder to be transferred concurrent with, or within ten days of receipt by SFY or MMG." SFY refers to the plaintiff, and MMG refers to defendant Harold A. Molitor and the Molitor Management Group.

9. None of the securities listed in the Severance Agreement were ever transferred by Molitor Management Group, Inc., or Harold Molitor to Stephen F. Yount.

10. On or about October 6, YR-4, Molitor Management Group, Inc., by its Chairman, Harold A. Molitor, and Harold A. Molitor, individually, signed a document with Stephen F. Yount entitled Amendment to Severance Agreement (the Amendment). The Amendment to the Severance Agreement provides, in relevant part, that:

> The original May 31, YR-4, date by which Harold Molitor was obligated to cause certain enumerated interests to be transferred to SFY has extended to January 31, YR-3. Harold Molitor will cause these enumerated interests to be transferred to SFY on or before January 31, YR-3. To the extent Harold Molitor or MMG do not yet have possession or control of these interests as of the date for transfer, Harold Molitor will cause those interests, or any remaining portion thereof, to be transferred to SFY within ten days of receipt by him or by MMG. All other terms of the Severance Agreement shall remain unchanged.

The Amendment to the Severance Agreement is incorporated by reference and is attached hereto as Exhibit 4.

11. To date, neither Molitor Management Group, Inc., nor Harold A. Molitor has transferred to the plaintiff any of the stock encompassed by the Severance Agreement and/or the Amendment.

COUNT I

Breach of Contract

Stephen F. Yount v. Molitor Management Group, Inc.

12. The plaintiff reincorporates and realleges paragraphs 1 through 11 as if fully set forth herein.

13. To date, Molitor Management Group, Inc., has failed to transfer any of the securities listed in the Severance Agreement and/or the Amendment to Severance Agreement to Stephen F. Yount.

14. As a result of the failure of Molitor Management Group, Inc., to deliver the securities to Stephen F. Yount, Molitor Management Group, Inc., is in breach of contract.

WHEREFORE, the plaintiff, Stephen F. Yount, demands judgment in his favor, together with interest, attorney fees, and costs.

COUNT II

Breach of Contract

Stephen F. Yount v. Harold A. Molitor

15. The plaintiff reincorporates and realleges paragraphs 1 through 14 as if fully set forth herein.

16. To date, Harold A. Molitor has failed to transfer any of the securities listed in the Severance Agreement and/or the Amendment to Severance Agreement to Stephen F. Yount.

17. As a result of the failure of Harold A. Molitor to deliver the securities to Stephen F. Yount, Harold A. Molitor is in breach of contract.

WHEREFORE, the plaintiff, Stephen F. Yount, demands judgment in his favor, together with interest, attorney fees, and costs.

COUNT III

Guarantee

Stephen F. Yount v. Harold A. Molitor

18. The plaintiff reincorporates and realleges paragraphs 1 through 17 as if fully set forth herein.

19. By signing the Severance Agreement and the Amendment to Severance Agreement in his individual capacity, Harold A. Molitor is the Guarantor of Molitor Management Group, Inc.'s, obligation under the two agreements.

20. The plaintiff has not received any of the securities that are the subject of the two agreements, and therefore Harold A. Molitor is liable to the plaintiff in his capacity as Guarantor as well as in his individual capacity.

WHEREFORE, the plaintiff, Stephen F. Yount, demands judgment in his favor, together with interest, attorney fees, and costs.

COUNT IV

Deceit

Stephen F. Yount v. Molitor Management Group, Inc.

21. The plaintiff reincorporates and realleges paragraphs 1 through 20 as if fully set forth herein.

22. Molitor Management Group, Inc., never had the intention to convey the securities in question or, in the alternative, acted with recklessness in ascertaining the truth or falsity of its representations.

23. Accordingly, Molitor Management Group, Inc., has committed the tort of deceit against the plaintiff and the plaintiff has been damaged thereby.

WHEREFORE, the plaintiff, Stephen F. Yount, demands judgment in his favor, together with interest, attorney fees, and costs.

COUNT V

Deceit

Stephen F. Yount v. Harold A. Molitor

24. The plaintiff reincorporates and realleges paragraphs 1 through 23 as if fully set forth herein.

25. Harold A. Molitor never had the intention to convey the securities in question or, in the alternative, acted with recklessness in ascertaining the truth or falsity of his representations.

26. Accordingly, Harold A. Molitor has committed the tort of deceit against the plaintiff and the plaintiff has been damaged thereby.

WHEREFORE, the plaintiff, Stephen F. Yount, demands judgment in his favor, together with interest, attorney fees, and costs.

Respectfully submitted,
Stephen F. Yount,

By his attorney,
MALLORY AND MORGAN

Pat Morgan
Pat Morgan
55 Memorial Drive
Nita City, Nita 01024
Date: May 1, YR-2
(555) 123-5705

PLAINTIFF DEMANDS A TRIAL BY JURY

STATE OF NITA

CENTRAL, ss.	SUPERIOR COURT CIVIL ACTION NO.

STEPHEN F. YOUNT,
Plaintiff

v.

MOLITOR MANAGEMENT GROUP, INC., And HAROLD A. MOLITOR
Defendants

ANSWER

The Defendant answers the complaint of Stephen F. Yount as follows:

PARTIES

1. The plaintiff in this matter is Stephen F. Yount, an individual who resides at 204 Seaview Court, Nita City, Nita 01532. **Admits.**

2. A defendant in this case is Molitor Management Group, Inc., a Nita corporation with offices located at 24 Yardley Executive Park, Yardley, Nita 01533. **Admits.**

3. A defendant in this case is Harold A. Molitor, an individual who resides at 55 Marbleridge Road, Topsfield, Nita, 01845. **Admits.**

STATEMENT OF THE CASE

4. As recently as YR-4, the plaintiff, Stephen F. Yount, was an employee of Molitor Management Group, Inc. **Admits.**

5. At all times relevant hereto, Harold A. Molitor was the Chairman of Molitor Management Group, Inc. **Admits.**

6. On or about April 30, YR-5, an agreement entitled Severance Agreement was entered into by and between Stephen F. Yount, Molitor Management Group, Inc., and Harold A. Molitor, individually (the Agreement). **Denies each and every allegation contained in paragraph 6.**

7. The Agreement provided, in relevant part, that "(i)n lieu of $7,212.00 owed to Stephen F. Yount (SFY) by Molitor Management Group, Inc. (MMG), SFY will purchase from MMG and Harold A. Molitor for set amount the following interests." The Agreement listed certain securities that were subject to the purchase. A true and complete copy of the Severance Agreement is attached hereto as Exhibit 1 and incorporated by reference. **Denies each and every allegation contained in paragraph 7.**

8. The Agreement further provided, after the list of securities, in relevant part, that "Harold Molitor will cause those interests above currently in his or MMG's possession to be transferred to SFY by May 31, YR-5, with the remainder to be transferred concurrent with, or within ten days of receipt by SFY or MMG." SFY refers to the plaintiff, and MMG refers to defendant Harold A. Molitor and the Molitor Management Group. **Denies each and every allegation contained in paragraph 8.**

9. None of the securities listed in the Severance Agreement were ever transferred by Molitor Management Group, Inc., or Harold Molitor to Stephen F. Yount. **Admits.**

10. On or about October 6, YR-4, Molitor Management Group, Inc., by its Chairman, Harold A. Molitor, and Harold A. Molitor, individually, signed a document with Stephen F. Yount entitled Amendment to Severance Agreement (the Amendment). The Amendment to the Severance Agreement provides, in relevant part, that:

> The original May 31, YR-5, date, by which Harold Molitor was obligated to cause certain enumerated interests to be transferred to SFY has extended to January 31, YR-3. Harold Molitor will cause these enumerated interests to be transferred to SFY on or before January 31, YR-3. To the extent Harold Molitor or MMG do not yet have possession or control of these interests as of the date for transfer, Harold Molitor will cause those interests, or any remaining portion thereof, to be transferred to SFY within ten days of receipt by him or by MMG. All other terms of the Severance Agreement shall remain unchanged.

The Amendment to the Severance Agreement is incorporated by reference and is attached hereto as Exhibit 4. **Denies each and every allegation contained in paragraph 10.**

11. To date, neither Molitor Management Group, Inc., nor Harold A. Molitor has transferred to the plaintiff any of the stock encompassed by the Severance Agreement and/or the Amendment. **Denies the allegation in paragraph 11 that there was any agreement for the transfer of stock.**

COUNT I

Breach of Contract

Stephen F. Yount v. Molitor Management Group, Inc.

12. The plaintiff reincorporates and realleges paragraphs 1 through 11 as if fully set forth herein. **Readmits and re-denies the same as listed above.**

13. To date, Molitor Management Group, Inc., has failed to transfer any of the securities listed in the Severance Agreement and/or the Amendment to Severance Agreement to Stephen F. Yount. **Admits.**

14. As a result of the failure of Molitor Management Group, Inc., to deliver the securities to Stephen F. Yount, Molitor Management Group, Inc. is in breach of contract. **Denies.**

COUNT II

Breach of Contract

Stephen F. Yount v. Harold A. Molitor

15. The plaintiff reincorporates and realleges paragraphs 1 through 14 as if fully set forth herein. **Readmits and re-denies as alleged above.**

16. To date, Harold A. Molitor has failed to transfer any of the securities listed in the Severance Agreement and/or the Amendment to Severance Agreement to Stephen F. Yount. **Denies there was any Severance Agreement between the Parties.**

17. As a result of the failure of Harold A. Molitor to deliver the securities to Stephen F. Yount, Harold A. Molitor is in breach of contract. **Denies.**

COUNT III

Guarantee

Stephen F. Yount v. Harold A. Molitor

18. The plaintiff reincorporates and realleges paragraphs 1 through 17 as if fully set forth herein. **Readmits and re-denies as alleged above.**

19. By signing the Severance Agreement and the Amendment to Severance Agreement in his individual capacity, Harold A. Molitor is the Guarantor of Molitor Management Group, Inc.'s, obligation under the two agreements. **Denies.**

20. The plaintiff has not received any of the securities that are the subject of the two agreements and, therefore, Harold A. Molitor is liable to the plaintiff in his capacity as Guarantor as well as in his individual capacity. **Denies there was any Severance Agreement between the Parties.**

COUNT IV

Deceit

Stephen F. Yount v. Molitor Management Group, Inc.

21. The plaintiff reincorporates and realleges paragraphs 1 through 20 as if fully set forth herein. **Readmits and re-denies as alleged above.**

22. Molitor Management Group, Inc., never had the intention to convey the securities in question or, in the alternative, acted with recklessness in ascertaining the truth or falsity of its representations. **Denies.**

23. Accordingly, Molitor Management Group, Inc. has committed the tort of deceit against the plaintiff and the plaintiff has been damaged thereby. **Denies.**

COUNT V

Deceit

Stephen F. Yount v. Harold A. Molitor

24. The plaintiff reincorporates and realleges paragraphs 1 through 23 as if fully set forth herein. **Readmits and re-denies as alleged above.**

25. Harold A. Molitor never had the intention to convey the securities in question or, in the alternative, acted with recklessness in ascertaining the truth or falsity of its representations. **Denies.**

26. Accordingly, Harold A. Molitor has committed the tort of deceit against the plaintiff and the plaintiff has been damaged thereby. **Denies.**

WHEREFORE, the DEFENDANT, HAROLD A. MOLITOR, demands judgment in his favor, together with interest, attorney fees and costs.

Respectfully submitted,
Harold A. Molitor,

By his attorney,
CONCEPCIÓN, NUNN & LANEY

Cris Concepción

Cris Concepción (244720)
17 Msgr. O'Brien Highway
Nita City, Nita 02141
Date: May 1, YR-2
(555) 122-9182

DEFENDANT DEMANDS A TRIAL BY JURY

Depositions

Deposition of Stephen Yount, August 15, YR-1

My name is Stephen F. Yount, Jr., but I go by "Fred," both personally and professionally. I am thirty-seven years old. I live at 204 Seaview Court, Nita City, Nita. I am single, divorced from my wife, Susan, as of June YR-2. I have no children.

I went to public schools for both elementary and high school. I was a good student. My dad owned a hardware store, and I grew up spending a lot of time helping out in the store. I was pretty sports crazy as a kid. I played both varsity basketball and baseball in high school. I went to college at University of Rhode Island (URI). I was a Sigma Chi, played intramural basketball and baseball, and generally had a good time. I got a BS in business in YR-15.

I went to work straight out of college for Harold (YR-15). He had been a Sigma Chi, too, but at Furman University, in South Carolina. He was a real basketball fan. He loved Duke. He was then running a small manufacturing plant in Nita that was owned by his wife's father. The place was called Tee Manufacturing. It made cotton t-shirts for L.L.Bean. I interviewed with Harold at a job fair at the end of my senior year, and I was hired as an administrative assistant/ bookkeeper.

Harold and I really hit it off. He was like a mentor to me. He taught me everything I knew about business. I had some basic accounting, so I did the books. We also put together a business plan for the plant expansion. He also taught me about investing.

He and I also were friends outside of work. We played some golf together and watched a good number of basketball games together during basketball season. We were also both Red Sox fans. After work we used to go to a local sports bar and hang out and watch the games.

We made some decent money in the market. We got lucky on a couple of penny stocks. He used to share with me a newsletter that he gotten on high-tech penny stocks. He said he was going to write his own newsletter someday.

In YR-12, Harold got caught cheating on his wife. He divorced. He also left his father-in-law's t-shirt business and bought his own manufacturing plant, called Cotton Tops. I went with him to his new manufacturing plant. Again, we manufactured a variety of t-shirts for various retailers.

It was around this same time that I got married to Susan Durham. I knew Susan from URI. She was from Nita City and had been working since college at a local retailer selling shoes. We had dated at URI and decided to live together after college. We were good for each other back then, and we decided to get married. Harold came to the wedding. He paid for our honeymoon.

All the while, Harold and I were investing in the stock market, mostly in penny stock. Harold became obsessed with penny stocks. I mostly broke even. At times, he seemed to hit it big. He decided, however, that the real money was in trading penny stock for others. We both got licensed.

As a result, we worked up a business plan to hire out-of-work brokers to work the phones and sell penny stock to investors. We tried out our business plan at the same time we were working at Cotton Tops. But it was clear that the calls needed to be made during the daytime, when people were at work, so Harold decided he would have to sell Cotton Tops if he was going to make a real go of the new business.

In YR-10, Harold sold Cotton Tops and took his money and rented an office space in downtown Nita. His idea was to be a trader of penny stock. He also started Molitor Technologies Fund so that he could also pick and choose various stocks to trade on his own account. He was also able to get some of his more moneyed acquaintances to become limited partners. I wasn't willing to buy into the investing side of the business. Despite this, he asked me to move with him to the new business, both to sell stock and also to help him keep the books.

In the first couple of years, Harold seemed to be doing great. Since I was doing the books, I knew the business was making some real money: around $1.3 million a year. He bought this great place on the river. It was like a Virginia plantation, with a great view and great backyard, a volleyball pit, and a manicured lawn down to the water. And while I was making more than I ever had, it was only about $85,000 a year, peanuts compared to Harold. Between the trading and the fund, we had a money-making machine.

Harold would pay callers about $20 an hour, plus a small commission to make calls. He had lists of investors from all over the country who had either invested in penny stock before or were invested in the technology industry. The brokers would call and sell stock over the phone. The stock was mostly stock of start-up companies, sold over the counter. Most of the stock we were selling sold for less than a dollar. He would get information on the various stocks and teach the callers what to say about each stock. Basically he would only give them positive stuff to say about the stock, so that if they were asked about any of the negative stuff, they honestly wouldn't know about it. I used to do it from time to time and got pretty good at it. You would know in a minute of two if you were going to make a sale. You could hear it in their voice that greed would take over. Some would risk buying thousands of dollars of stock, dreaming that they were going to get rich. You could make thousands of dollars on the sale, if they bought a lot of it. Most times, the caller would just make a few dollars' investment.

Sometime in YR-6, it started to get harder and harder to sell stock. The tech bubble burst, and most of our customers had lost most of their money. They were in no mood to buy more stock. Harold was hopeful that things would yet turn around. He encouraged me to go to a couple of sessions to learn about buying and selling option contracts. He also had me go to the Bahamas to learn about investing offshore. He thought it would be good for me to diversify my understanding of investing. I went to these conferences based on the promise from Harold that he would pick up my expenses. That is how I incurred the approximately $7,200 in expenses.

In April YR-5, Harold said he could not pay my salary any more. He told me that I would have to make my money on commissions from selling stock. I tried for a while, but it was impossible.

It was during this time that I also got a call from the SEC asking about the business. The FBI also came by one day, but Harold turned them away and told me not to talk with them without his attorney being present. I started to look for another job.

At the end of April, I confronted Harold with a demand that he pay my travel expenses or I was going to leave. He pleaded with me to stick it out to the end of the year, when he was sure things would turn around. I told him I wanted a severance agreement. It was at this point that he suggested he give me the stocks that we listed in the agreement in lieu of the expenses. He also said it was his showing of good faith, giving me shares of his best stocks. I know he claims he used the word "gift," but we both knew he was trying to keep me working there. I took his promise as satisfaction for the travel expenses that I had incurred.

Susan and I were living off of her salary at this time, and she was getting pretty frustrated. I guess she was right that I was blind to Harold's real situation. We both had enjoyed Harold's largess over the years. Like I said, Harold paid for our honeymoon. In addition, he always bought the tickets if we were going to a ballgame, and he picked up lunch hundreds of times. We spent countless evenings together on his back patio at his riverfront house. Part of his way of entertaining was that we would drink expensive bottles of wine. There is no doubt he was generous to me over the years, though he never cut me in on any of the real money he was making.

Finally, in the summer of YR-5, I lined up a job working at a local bank and stopped coming in all together. Harold agreed to sign the severance agreement that May. But then he never paid up. We still hung out once in a while after work and on weekends. I guess you could say we remained friends. Yes, Exhibit 1 is the original severance agreement.

Ever since I left Molitor Technology Fund, my wife was hounding me to make Harold pay up. One night in late September YR-4, we went over to his house. I had promised Susan that I would ask him for the money, but the opportunity never presented itself. As to the incident he says happened at his house that night, I don't know what he is talking about. I guess I wouldn't have put it past Susan. I remember she was pretty unhappy with me. It is just that I don't remember anything happening that night that was unusual. Yes, Exhibit 1 is the original severance agreement.

Then, on October 6, YR-4, I went in to Harold with a typed-out amended severance agreement. I tried to get Harold to sign it. It was on a Friday, at the end of the day. It was just the two of us. His secretary may have come in at one point. He was upset that I had left. He said that he still thought things would turn around. There were all these new applications in the market (games and social media) and plenty of penny stock businesses coming on the market. I said I was done. That my marriage was on the rocks, and my wife was angry at me and won't rest till I got paid what was owed me.

He said he still thought there was good value in a couple of the listed stocks in our severance agreement. He showed me his newsletter to his limited partners as proof that Standard TECH had good value. Harold said he thought it was worth well over $100,000. I told him TelexGlobal was restricted stock and that it was worthless to me. He would have to release the restrictions. He told me that it would be easy for him to do. I told him I had heard it all before. I wanted it in writing. He asked me if I didn't trust him. I something like, "It isn't that I don't trust you, but Susan is adamant that I demand what I'm entitled to." I can see this copy of the amendment isn't signed, but that doesn't mean he didn't agree [Exhibit 4]. I knew he would try this. That is why I took a picture of the signed document with my cell phone [Exhibit 5]. Yes, when I got home, I made a copy of it for my files. I know it is not dated. I just emailed it to myself, saved it in my photos, and then printed out a copy. This is a copy I gave to my attorney.

In any event, when I made my copy, I also sent one to Susan. I made a screenshot and then pressed the share application. Then I then emailed it to her.

I got to thinking that I would like to have a signed copy from Harold, so I sent him a blank one and asked him to send it back to me. I understand now that Harold says he never got it. Until the lawsuit, he never denied having signed it, or getting it back from me, or agreeing to the amendment. Good thing Susan kept a copy of what I sent her [Exhibit 7].

Q: When did you send her this photo of Molitor's signature?

A: Well, I don't remember exactly. I have a vague memory she was demanding to see the signed copy. I wasn't exactly sure how to send it to her at the time. It was a new phone, and I was still getting used to . . . learning how to send photos. I might not have sent it until the next day.

He still hasn't paid me back my expenses or delivered any of the stock that he promised that he would deliver to me.

I worked for a while for SunTrust Bank. I started as a bank teller making $10 an hour. Then I became a branch manager, making $75,000 a year. Now I have taken over the family hardware store. My dad is recently retired, and I am gradually buying him out.

Susan left me shortly after I started with SunTrust. I guess the frustrations from not getting paid and then the loss of my salary were just too much for her. She married her boss from the shoe store.

Deposition of Susan Durham, August 17, YR-1

Current Status

My name is Susan A. Durham. I am thirty-five years old. I was born and went to elementary school and high school in Nita. I went to college at University of Rhode Island and graduated in YR-15. I received a BS degree in business. I met Fred Yount at URI. He followed me back home to Nita City after college, and we lived together for a while before we were married in YR-13. We divorced two years ago. As part of our divorce, we agreed that we would split the proceeds of his severance agreement with Harold Molitor and Molitor Technologies.

I was represented by Lee Bailey for my divorce. I am not currently represented by any attorney concerning this matter.

Background and Early Years of Marriage

After graduation from URI, I was really sick of school. I took the summer off and then got a job in a high-end shoe store selling shoes. I was really good at it and was able to make close to $60,000 selling shoes. That was big money for me at the time. Fred went to work straight out of college for Mr. Molitor (YR-15). They really seemed to hit it off. Fred and Harold were both Sigma Chis. They both loved sports and golf. Fred worked for Mr. Molitor in a business called Tee Manufacturing. It made cotton t-shirts for L.L.Bean. Fred had interviewed with Mr. Molitor at a job fair at the end of his senior year and was hired as an administrative assistant/bookkeeper.

Fred and I lived together for a couple of years. We were at ease with each other, and both of us made good money, so we spent fairly freely, took vacations, and ate out a lot.

In YR-12, Mr. Molitor got caught cheating on his wife. He got a divorce. He also left the t-shirt place and bought his own manufacturing plant, this time called Cotton Tops. Fred went with him to his new manufacturing plant. They manufactured a variety of t-shirts for various retailers and spent a lot of time together during this time. Strangely enough, seeing how devastated Mr. Molitor was about his divorce made us think about getting married. It was six months after Fred went to work at Cotton Tops that Fred and I got married. Mr. Molitor came to the wedding. He also paid for our honeymoon.

We had about five years where things were going pretty well for us. I knew that Mr. Molitor was restless because he was investing in the stock market, mostly in penny stock. Mr. Molitor became obsessed with penny stocks. He got Fred to invest also. At times, he seemed to hit it big. Harold decided, however, that the real money was in trading penny stock for others. They worked up this business plan to hire desperate, out-of-work brokers to work the phones and sell penny stock to investors. They tried it for a while at the same time Fred was working at Cotton Tops. But it was clear that the calls needed to be made during the daytime, when people were at work, so something would have to give if they were going to make the brokerage business work.

In YR-10, Mr. Molitor sold Cotton Tops and took his money and rented office space in downtown Nita. Despite my protests, Fred decided to go with him. I wanted him to stay with Cotton Tops and work for Mr. Mallory. Between us, we were taking in over $155,000 a year. We had bought a nice home in a great neighborhood, and while our mortgage was high, we still had enough money for eating out and plenty of travel. We also bought a sailboat, which I just loved. We had to sell it when things turned bad in YR-5.

Bahamas Trip

In February of YR-5, Fred came home and said that Harold wanted him to go to a high-tech conference in the Bahamas. Fred said Harold wanted him to prospect for some new technology companies and learn more about the industry. Business was already bad at Molitor, and Fred's pay had been cut substantially. I admit I was encouraging Fred to leave and see if he could go back to work for Cotton Tees, or get a job in a bank, or do something where he could bring in some money. Things were getting tough for us a number of fronts. We had tried to renegotiate our mortgage, which was originally a subprime mortgage, only to learn that our mortgage was now more than our house was worth. I was getting really sick of selling shoes and was eager to go back to school to get an MBA. But that was not in the cards. My parents' health was also failing. My dad had a heart attack, and my mom was showing signs of early dementia. I was spending a lot of time taking care of them. I was trying to get them in a long-term care facility, but it was hard to find them one they could afford.

Fred said we needed to get away to sort things out, and the Bahamas sounded like a nice break. Fred told me Harold had agreed to pick up the whole trip. We went first class. We had a suite. We put it on our credit card. Fred never got reimbursed.

I'll admit, we had a great time. We had great dinners, went scuba diving, and rented a little sailboat. We took long walks on the beach, and it looked like we were going to make some real changes. Fred said he was going to leave Molitor Technologies and look for a new job. He said he was going to tell Harold he was leaving when he got back.

I don't think that Fred went to very much of the conference. We spent most of our time there together.

Severance Agreement

It turned out it would take Fred longer to leave than either of us had hoped. Fred's excuse was that he was going to stay until he got the travel expenses reimbursed. Then, in April YR-5, Mr. Molitor said he couldn't pay Fred any salary any more, but that he would have to make his money on commissions, from selling stock. When I heard this, I hit the roof.

Fred next told me he owed it to Harold to stay because Harold was getting some heat from the government about the whole penny stock business. Fred swore to me he wasn't doing anything wrong, but he didn't know about what Harold was doing on the investing side of the business. We had long felt uneasy about whether Harold was selling his losing stock to the customers who were being cold called.

Finally, at the end of April, Fred confronted Mr. Molitor with a demand that he pay the travel expenses or he was going to leave. Fred told me that Harold suggested instead giving us some of his best stock in lieu of the expenses. Fred said he was giving us shares of his best stocks. The value would more than pay off our mortgage and really take the pressure off.

I admit that I wanted to believe that it was true, too. We were living off of my salary at this time, and I was getting pretty frustrated carrying the whole load by myself. We both had enjoyed the largess of Mr. Molitor over the years. He had paid for our honeymoon, and we spent countless evenings together on his back patio at his riverfront house. He would always pick up and pay for tickets at sporting events, and meals, and was always buying expensive bottles of wine. There is no doubt he was generous to us over the years.

Finally, in the summer of YR-5, Fred lined up a job working at a local bank and stopped working for Molitor Technology. Fred showed me the severance agreement Harold signed, and I put it in our important papers. But then he never paid up. We all still hung out once in a while after work and on weekends. I guess you could say we remained friends.

Ever since Fred left Molitor Technology, I was on Fred to make Harold pay up. It drove me crazy to have that on our credit card and to be paying 14 percent interest on the money. One night, in late September YR-4, we went over to his house. Fred had promised me that that night he would ask Harold for the money, but I guess the opportunity never presented itself.

I don't really remember much of what happened that night. I had too much wine. I know we went swimming. I may have been flirting with Harold some. He is a charming guy.

I do remember visiting Harold's Facebook page after the party and was horrified to see a picture of me and Fred, looking pretty drunk. I don't remember commenting on the picture, but I may have. I do remember getting an email about it from Harold [Exhibit 3] afterward, which I saved in my email. As you can see, he was pretty inappropriate and I deny I ever propositioned him. Fortunately, he took down that embarrassing photo. In any event, he said that he would take care of us and make up the hard times that we had gone through together.

Severance Extension

I know that Fred was livid that Harold had not delivered the stock as he had promised. After the night at the house, he went to confront Harold. I think it was early October. He had typed up an amended severance agreement with an extension for delivery of the stock. Fred told me that he went to Mr. Molitor with amended severance agreement. He tried to get Mr. Molitor to sign it. I do know that he left me a text message as he left his meeting with Harold saying, "Harold agreed!" When he got home I asked to see the signed agreement. He at first hesitated. Then he said, I have better than that. I took a picture of the signed agreement with my cell phone. I told him to send it to me. I think he got around to sending it the next day. Exhibit 7 is a copy. I kept it on my cell, and it was dated October 7 at 2:05 p.m.

As to his message coming out of the meeting, that is the text message I got. Yes, he must have kept a copy. Yes, I remember getting it on October 6 at around 2:00 p.m.

When he got home, I know I saw him make a copy of something and then put it in an envelope. He said it was for Harold, to show he had a picture of the signed severance agreement extension. That is all I know.

We still haven't been paid back our expenses or were given any of the stocks that Harold promised he would deliver to us. Fred worked for a while for SunTrust Bank. He started as a bank teller making $10 an hour. Then he became a branch manager, making $75,000 a year. But he just was not happy there. It was pretty tough on both of us.

I left Fred shortly after he started with SunTrust. I am now remarried to Jim Chilcutt, who was my boss from the shoe store.

I understand that Fred has taken over the family hardware store. His dad is recently retired, and Fred is gradually buying him out.

Deposition of Harold Molitor, July 31, YR-1

My name is Harold Molitor. I am fifty-nine years old. My father was a law partner in a big firm in New York. Dad divorced my mom when I was seven. I had very few dealings with my father after he divorced my Mom. My dad passed away about ten years ago. I inherited $1 million from his estate. I used my inheritance to buy my home on the river.

When my mom got divorced, we moved back to her home in Richmond, Virginia. She remarried. I grew up going to private schools. I went to St. Christopher's High School, an Episcopal high school. I played baseball in high school. I went to Furman College in South Carolina. I played baseball there. I tried out for the Detroit Tigers, but was never drafted.

I met a girl when I was a student at Furman from Nita City. We fell in love and got married right out of college (YR-37). Her father took me into the family businesses. My father-in-law had a number of manufacturing businesses and turned one of them over to me. It was a small manufacturing business. We manufactured cotton t-shirts for L.L.Bean. It was called Tee Manufacturing.

But he didn't just give it to me. I first was a management trainee for a year. Then I was made the floor manager. I was pretty good with the employees. I knew everyone by name and knew their family situations. They even came to me for advice about a lot of things. It was like we were family. I guess those were the best times I had in business, though I didn't know it at the time.

The employees punched the clock. Our benefits and pay were good enough to keep the union from coming in. Like I said, it was a small factory, with only about thirty employees. Still, the payroll was over a half-million a year, and you had to keep on top of things if you were going to make any money.

I learned the business from the ground up. I knew how to keep the books, how to bid jobs, and how to manage our relationship with L.L.Bean. Our competitors were trying to take our book of business away all the time, so we had to stay on our toes and keep our pricing competitive. Still, at some point, it became sort of routine. I know I played a lot of golf, including Wednesday afternoons, Fridays, and Sundays. But that started to get old.

Then, after about ten years of running the business, I started to get more and more interested in investing. At first, I invested in a very diversified portfolio. Then I really started to focus on high-tech companies. I was pretty good at picking stocks (though you would have had to be an idiot not to make money for a while there, as tech was really hot). I made enough to put away a nice nest egg to protect our future.

Once I had set aside a couple hundred thousand, I started to invest in penny stock. I set aside a pot of money that I could lose. I called it my "mad money." I never lost it all, but never really hit it big either. I came to learn that the money to be made in penny stock was more in the trading side of the business. My broker buddies were making good money. There always seemed to be investors out there willing to try to make a quick buck. Whether they picked a good stock or a bad one, they would have to pay the trading fees. This was before online brokerages, and so you could make $30 to $100 dollars on a trade, depending on the number and value of the shares bought or sold.

Anyway, I got really interested in trading stock. I got some friends of mine from college who ran a local brokerage business to sponsor me. I took and passed my series 7 Financial Industry Regulation Authority (FINRA) exam. I also passed the Nita series 6 exam and became a licensed broker. While I was still full time at the "Tee" business, I advertised myself as a specialist in trading penny stock. I started a newsletter for my customers soon thereafter.

In YR-15, I started to think about hiring someone who I could teach to run Tee Manufacturing so I could spend more time on the brokerage business. I went to a college fair at URI, and met Stephen Yount. He goes by Fred. He and I really hit it off.

My wife and I had been trying to have kids, but nothing ever worked out. I was skittish about adopting. Friends of mine who adopted always seemed to get more than they bargained for. Anyway, maybe I was looking for more than an employee when I hired Yount. And I have to say, for a while, he was like the son I never had. He introduced me to his fiancée. We used to have them over all the time. When they got married, his dad didn't come to the wedding, so I stepped in and played the role. I paid for the rehearsal dinner. I even paid for his honeymoon.

I used to have him out to my lake house all the time. We would go boating, water skiing, have drinks. We played some golf. As bad as I was, he was worse.

About two years after Fred started to work for me, I really made a stupid mistake. I had an affair with a woman I met when I was studying for my brokerage license. And when I tried to end it, she went and told my wife about the affair. My wife booted me out of the house, and we ended up getting a divorce. I felt really guilty about the whole thing. As part of the divorce settlement, my wife got the house and the nest egg I had saved up. I decided to sell my interest in Tee Manufacturing and buy another small manufacturing business, but outside of the family business. This one was called Cotton Tees. I bought Cotton Tees in YR-13.

I owned Cotton Tees for about two years. It provided me with some new cash to start Molitor Technologies. Fred kept the books at Cotton Tees and was very helpful in running the plant. I lined up various jobs. We made custom t-shirts. Different groups would send in a design, or pick one from a stock set we had, and then we would produce them. We made decent money. Nothing spectacular. Then I got a nice offer from my ex-father in law to buy me out. I decided to take it and went all-in on the brokerage business. It was then I started Molitor Technologies Fund.

I talked Fred into coming with me. He and I had been working together investing and trading penny stock, both for our account and for other traders. He even worked some late afternoons making sales calls. I would work up an information sheet on a company, and then we would call our prospects and pitch the stock.

When we went all in on selling penny stock, we decided we needed a bright, cheap labor force. We hired brokers who had no book of business and had been out of work for months. They were desperate. We were able to get a great group of ten to fifteen sales people. They would be given a sheet on the companies we were recommending. They would make the sales pitch and get a percentage of the brokerage fees if they made a sale.

I also decided to set up a partnership for buying and selling the stock. My limited partners would participate in the profits and losses that Molitor Technologies made in the market. Sometimes we would pitch stock to prospects that the Fund was trying to sell. The sales force never knew anything about the stock, other than what I provided them, so they were clean regarding the partnership side of the business. I always kept a good Chinese wall between the sales force and the partnership.

We made real good money for a while. I might have made over a million dollars in YR-7. But then the tech bubble burst and things started to deteriorate. First, the cold calling just dried up. Next, we started to get competition from online trading businesses with very low trading fees. In YR-6, we were able to break even. But then, in YR-5, it was just Fred and me, trying to keep it going. I started to think about going online myself.

I admit that during this time we were pretty desperate to unload some of our positions. Some of our customers must have complained. In YR-5, we were investigated by the state regulators. No, I wasn't running a boiler room. We never lied to anyone. We may not have always told them everything there was to know about the stock, but we always told them what was public information. Anyone trading in penny stock knows the risks are high that the businesses will fail.

And don't let Fred fool you. He knew exactly what was going on. He knew the business model. He knew we were making money on the trades. He may not have known everything about the limited partnership, but he knew we were selling stock that we once owned ourselves.

I deny we were running a "boiler room." I don't even know what that is. Sure, we played on the greed of investors to make money fast in penny stock. Between YR-10 and YR-5, I made an average of about $800,000 a year.

Here was the idea behind Molitor Technologies Fund: over the years we also built up a class of investors that liked to make fast money. I had about twenty limited partners. They each put in $250,000. Again, for a while, we were returning about twenty percent a year to the limited partners. Then, in YR-5, we started to tank, and by the end of YR-4 we all lost it all. I lived on my savings for a while until I could start up something new.

Yes, I did write a newsletter to my limited partners, keeping them up on the values of the stocks we held. I understand it would have been illegal for me to make any misrepresentations to them about those stocks.

In a way, I was expecting it when Fred came in to talk in April of YR-5. Since January that year, I had told Fred I couldn't pay him salary, but had to just pay him commissions on trades. I know this was putting a lot of stress on his marriage. His wife had a good job, and they weren't going to lose their house or anything. They didn't have any kids, so they were getting by. I would pick up meals, and take the two of them out for dinner when I could. And they would come out to the lake house for dinner about once a month. We would drink wine and grill some steaks.

In any event, he said he had to look for another job. He told me his wife was on him about not contributing to the family income. I told him I thought that there were some new opportunities in social media start-ups. Everyone was making applications and games for the new iPhone. I thought we would be able to start to sell again.

I was also working on putting our business online. That way we could reach our prospects with emails. While the trading fees would be lower, there could be more of them. In an effort to show my good faith and give him something to tell his wife, I agreed to give him some shares that I owned through the limited partnership. But it was a gift, nothing more. By that point, it was clear he was leaving, so it wasn't like it was something he was working for. In addition, he agreed to the terms of work since last April, so it wasn't like I was paying him for that.

In October of YR-4, he came back to talk about my getting him the stock I promised to give him in May YR-5. This followed an event at the lake house. I am not sure, but I think what prompted his visit was what had occurred the weekend before. It was late September, and we went to the lake house for one last party before it turned cold. We all—Fred, Susan, and I—got pretty drunk. We went skinny dipping. Susan came on to me. I rebuffed her. Everyone was pretty embarrassed. The next Monday, Fred called and said he really needed to cut ties with me. He said that he really needed to get the stock I promised him. I think he was just really embarrassed and was trying to save a little face. And she commented on a photo I posted on Facebook. Exhibit 2 is a screenshot I went back and made of my Facebook (http://bit.ly/1Dv2ecl). I don't see her comment, but I remember it. "Hal, quite a night and a lot of great wine. Hope I behaved. Ugh!" Yes, that is my email I sent her after she posted her comment. Exhibit 3. It is what it is.

He came in on a Friday. He put the amended agreement in front of me. Yes. Exhibit 4 is what he tried to get me to sign. I told him I wasn't going to sign anything, that whatever we agreed, he could trust me. I told him that if I gave him my word, then I would deliver. But I reminded him the values of the stocks we listed were questionable. He said something mature like, "But you promised!" And I said, "You knew you were just getting in the same boat as everyone else. Most are restricted penny stocks!" I know he says otherwise, but I never promised him anything more than what we had agreed to before. And that was a gift, if anything at all. He left without getting anything in writing.

Q: Did you ever say or do anything to give the impression you were extending the agreement?

A: At one point, I may have made a show of air-signing my name across a piece of paper. I don't remember if it was on the agreement itself or otherwise. It probably was. In any event, he left with the agreement. I certainly never saw him take out his cell phone or take a picture of anything. No, I don't recognize my signature on Exhibits 5 or 7. I think he must have

Photoshopped it. And I never got his amended agreement back in the mail. If I had, I would have called him and told him I tore it up.

Molitor Technology Fund liquidated in YR-3. I now run a new business, with a similar format, under a new name, Molitor Online Technologies. It is again profitable. I made about $200,000 last year. I turned out to be right about the online business in penny stocks. I run it out of my home and make money on the trades. I work from my lakefront home. It was recently appraised at over $2 million.

Yes, Exhibit 1 is a copy of a writing I intended as a gift I made to Fred, but it was never meant as a contract or a binding agreement.

Yes, Exhibits 8 and 9 are stock certificates of stock MMG owned during YR-5, YR-4, and YR-3. They are now worthless.

Yes, Exhibit 10 is a copy of my balance sheet dated December 31, YR-4.

Yes, Exhibit 11 is a newsletter I prepared for my partners reporting on our holdings. It contains future predictions of both what we hope will happen in companies we own and in the value of the stock we hold. Predictions are just that: predictions. They are not statements of facts or meant to be relied on for making financial decisions.

Deposition of Melissa Still, July 30, YR-1

Background

My name is Melissa Still. I am fifty-five years old. I went to Nita High and graduated in YR-27. In high school, I was on the women's softball team and sang in the glee club. While I was a good student, people in my family did not go to a fancy liberal arts college. I graduated from Nita Community College with an associate's degree. I was a straight-A student. I graduated in YR-26.

I went to work for Mr. Mallory (my current boss's father-in-law) and worked for him till YR-13, when I left with Harold. Harold left Tee Manufacturing and started Cotton Tops Manufacturing. Harold talked me into staying with him again when he sold Cotton Tops and started his stock trading business, Molitor Technologies Fund, in YR-11. I have stayed with Harold through the good and the bad. We went out of business at one point and then he reopened his trading business as an online brokerage business in YR-2. This business is called Molitor Online Technology Fund. I still work for him today.

Since I moved with Harold to Cotton Tops in YR-13, I became almost like an office manager for Harold. He paid me very well, but also gave me a lot of responsibility. I was virtually running Cotton Tops for Harold in the last couple of years of its existence. He told me at the time he found the business boring, and he was spending more and more time on selling and trading high-tech penny stocks.

I was being paid close to $200,000 toward the end of my time at Cotton Tees. I worked with the customers—whether college kids looking to sell t-shirts for a fundraiser or big retailers looking to sell high-quality cotton t-shirts under their particular brand. I also did most of the book work. I dealt with our floor manager when Harold was out, which was most of time. The floor manager supervised the employees who made the t-shirts. We were a nonunion shop, so we had to deal with employee issues directly. We had about thirty employees total, both full and part time, and the payroll was about $500,000. Most of our full-time employees had worked for Mr. Mallory back before Cotton Tops. Harold, in fact, sold Cotton Tops back to Mr. Mallory, so most of these employees kept their jobs.

I first met Fred Yount when Harold hired him in YR-15, back when it was still Tee Manufacturing. I think Harold told Fred he was being groomed to run the business, but I think Harold was looking for someone he could play with. They both liked baseball and golf and spent more time out of the office at the sports bar than in the office. Fred was a nice enough guy, but never developed into someone Harold could trust to actually run things. Like I said, they played a lot of golf and watched a lot sports. The same was true after Harold got divorced and started Cotton Tops. He and Fred spent a lot of time together immediately before and after his divorce. I kind of felt sorry for Harold around then. He knew he had really screwed up his marriage. I think he might have leaned on young Fred a little too much during that time. I think it might have cost Fred some with his own wife to have to spend so much time with Harold.

Harold must have done pretty well with Cotton Tees because he told me that when he sold it to Mr. Mallory, he cleared about one million. Harold was itching to start something completely different. He had been studying for his brokerage license before he sold Cotton Tops, and when he got his license, he decided he was going to set up his own brokerage and sell high-tech stock. He persuaded me that we would do very well with it, and it would be great fun. I was in my mid-forties at the time, and my husband was a high school principal. While our kids were going off to college, we had been good savers and had set aside money for their tuition. I talked it over with my husband and decided that I could take the risk and stay with Harold. So I went with him to the new brokerage business. My main responsibility at first was to help hire the callers who were going to sell the stocks.

I call them "my kids," because many of them were the age of my kids. We had lists of prospective customers who had bought stock with us before or had been referred by other clients. In the mornings, Harold and I would draft up a statement on a particular stock and give it to the kids for them to use in making their sales pitch. Harold would have market data on the stock, and we would edit it to try to emphasize why the time was right for it to be purchased.

At first, Molitor Technologies Fund did pretty well. There was a technology boom in stocks at the time, and there were a large number of garage and basement start-ups trying to raise money. But after the boom, there was a bust. It started to turn in YR-6, but from YR-5 through YR-2, it was tough going. We eventually went out of business for a couple of months in YR-2, but then reopened after the economy turned around.

At first, Fred seemed pretty much along for the ride. He was not very good at selling stock. He just didn't have the passion for it. Harold tried to get Fred to help research and identify new start-ups and write them up, but he never really found much outside what Harold found on the Internet.

Bahamas

Harold did send Fred to a technology conference in the Bahamas to try to get him more of an understanding of start-ups in the technology industry. This was in February of YR-5. Fred took his wife along. They hadn't had a vacation in a long while. Harold was feeling generous, and it wouldn't surprise me if he told Fred he would pick up the bill. But I'm sure Harold also told Fred he would have to go to the meetings. Fred and his wife ran up quite a bill. It was over $7,000. I remember it included the cost of two first-class airplane tickets. They stayed in a suite.

I remember that when Fred got back, he submitted the receipts to me. I was livid about it, as I knew we didn't have the cash flow to be extravagant. I asked Fred about the charges, and he got huffy with me. He told me that Harold had promised to pick up the bill. I said I really didn't think Harold had intended to pick up first-class tickets or a suite. Fred told me it was the least Harold could do, what with the little Fred was being paid. Fred told me he was going to have to leave Molitor Tech because his wife was insisting that he make more money. Fred also told me as an aside that he didn't attend any of the meetings because his wife was very upset about his work, and she was insistent that he spend time with her.

When I told Harold what Fred had said, it was the first time I really saw Harold get mad at Fred. He told me not to pay the bill, that Fred had gone back on his promise to attend the meetings. So I threw the receipts into file and never reimbursed him. When he would ask after it, I told him that he needed to take it up with Harold. In any event, I checked the file, and I must have pitched it when Fred left the firm.

I really don't know anything about the other side of the business, the limited partnership. I also don't know anything about the newsletter. Harold handled that himself.

You have shown me the severance agreement dated in May YR-5. I don't know much about that. I do know that Fred came in to talk to Harold in April of YR-5. Harold later told me that Fred told him then that he needed to find another job. Apparently, Fred told Harold that he was going to keep working till he found another job, but wanted to let Harold know he was looking. He also insisted on a severance agreement. He said the pressure was just too great at home. And it had been close to eighteen months since he had brought home any significant money. Harold told me he felt for Fred, so he gave him some stock. He told me at the time the stock was not worth much of anything.

Starting in YR-4, Harold was working on putting our business online. He thought that once the online business started, we all would be back in the green. Fred said he just couldn't take the chance. I decided to wait it out and see.

I do know that on October 6 of YR-4, Fred came back to talk to Harold about getting him the stock Harold had apparently promised to give him in May YR-5. I remember Fred came in on a Friday. I was in the office doorway when Fred put the amended agreement in front of Harold. Harold told him he wasn't going to sign anything, that whatever they agreed to, Fred could trust Harold. They then had a pretty heated exchange. I may have turned away at some point to get something at my desk, but it could not have been for long. When I returned, Harold may have made a show of signing something. What I am absolutely sure of is that Fred did not have his cell phone out at the time. I didn't see him take a picture of any document. Fred then left, and as far as I remember, Fred didn't take anything with him when he left.

When Fred went past me, I remember putting my hands on my hips, as if to say to Harold, "You're not going to sign that, are you?" Harold said, "What the hell." In any event, I don't remember ever putting anything in the file, one way or another.

I'm pretty sure we never got a letter from Fred following that meeting in October. I would have been the one to get it if it was addressed to Harold. I always get Harold's mail, open it, and then respond to it when Harold tells me what to do. I can tell you I never made a copy of any signed agreement for our files. The one copy I saw was the one Fred left Harold when he stormed out. I have searched our files, and I didn't see a signed agreement or an unsigned agreement.

I can see you are showing me Exhibits 5 and 7. Yes, it probably is Harold's signature. That is the way he makes his M's and G's. But who knows whether it was Photoshopped. I can't tell when or where this photo is taken.

Molitor Technology Fund liquidated in YR-3. I now work with Harold in a new business. It has a similar format, but operates under a new name, Molitor Online Technologies Fund. It is again profitable. I made about $100,000 last year. I hope I will be up to my previous salary levels soon.

Expert Depositions, Reports, and CVs

Summary of Deposition of Plaintiff's Expert—Sam F. Singley

Went through credentials. Only recently has entered litigation support work, though did provide expert opinions before in anti-trust cases and securities fraud cases while still a professor at Nita State University. As an academic economist, studied the stock market throughout career. Since retirement, started own consulting business. Recently has been employed by the court to provide services as a conservator, special master, receiver, independent expert.

Employed by attorney for Yount. The attorney has used the expert before, but the expert had no previous contact with Yount.

Expert has dealt with a number of different stock valuation matters, but never had a chance to evaluate restricted stock. Experience with the market for restricted stock derived from discussions with the expert's uncle, who sold restricted stock in a start-up high tech that the uncle had owned. Is familiar with research tools that can be used to help determine the market value of restricted stock. Usually would have used the net asset value method and examined company books and balance sheets, but such a method is not reliable when applied to a start-up with little history of earnings.

Expert was given a copy of the contract between the parties and reviewed it. Is familiar with the contract between the parties, and its extension.

Expert was employed by attorney for Yount in April of YR-1, before the case was filed.

Expert talked with Yount's attorney directly about expert's understanding of the value of the stocks that were listed in the agreement. Expert agrees that Molitor's own newsletter contains statements of the value of two of the listed stocks that is very important to determining their value. Expert said would conduct own research into the companies in question, but also asked for any news or public information on the value of TelexGlobal.

Attorney showed the expert the NY AG's press release concerning TelexGlobal and was told that the release occurred after the time designated in the agreement for the stock to have been delivered to Yount. Expert verified this by checking the dates in the agreement and the press release. Expert did consult stock trades of TelexGlobal restricted stock in the months preceding the AG press release. Didn't find any record of any actual trades that had occurred during that time. Expert is quick to point out that 10Kwizard did indicate there was a bid and an ask price for TelexGlobal restricted stock and that it changed. This indicated to the expert that people were buying and selling, as the price changes should reflect actual buy and sells over the 10Kwizard system. (Singley determined that no TelexGlobal officers traded their stock during that time. The expert did not check with Molitor to see if he tried to sell his shares during that time.)

Counsel didn't give expert any publicly available financial information on TelexGlobal, nor did the expert discover any other news stories other than repeats of the AG's press release.

Singley was directed by counsel to restrict the valuation to two stocks, TelexGlobal and Nevada Software Standard TECH. Singley did not review publicly available information on these listed stocks over the relevant time period, as Molitor himself had valued these shares in his newsletter.

[*Authors' note: The following are interview notes that are to be considered as given in confidence, and are meant to raise a number of issues for discussion of ethical issues in working with experts.*]

In the expert's first draft of the report were the following statements.

"Valuing restricted stock is, at best, a guess, when there are no actual sales of such restricted stock that have occurred during the relevant time frame. The reason for this uncertainty is that the value of the stock depends on a number of variables, including 1) the willingness of restricted stock owners to sell their stock (usually whether the owner has access to cash to cover his other expenses), and 2) the number of and notice to potential buyers of the reasons the restricted stock owner wants to sell his or her stock."

After consulting with counsel, these sentences in their entirety were deleted from the report.

In addition, the expert disclosed the following to counsel:

Singley revealed that the language Singley used in the draft was taken from an earlier expert report rendered in arbitration. That arbitration was for *Krauledat v. Harvard Bioscience* and is listed in Singley's résumé. In that case, Singley had opined that the debtor's reliance on the market value of restricted stock he owned was misplaced, as it had no market value. At the time Singley gave that opinion, Singley had not conducted any research into the market for restricted stock. Singley was also not familiar at that time of the existence of 10Kwizard, and doesn't know whether the report or testimony were ever made public. Singley doubts it—doesn't think there was a court reporter at the arbitration, nor has Singley ever seen any public filing from that proceeding.

After consulting with counsel, it was determined that even though friends and family of officers and directors were often the purchasers of restricted stock, sometimes a market for such stock could arise through recommendations by other independent evaluators of the business. Molitor may have been a friend of officers of TelexGlobal, but the expert had no way of contacting Molitor to determine how he came to hold the TelexGlobal stock. In any event, Singley agreed that the existence of the 10Kwizard listings indicated a market for restricted stock that was not dependent on whether friends or family had access to information about the reasons the holder wanted to sell his or her securities. Counsel directed Singley that counsel would decide whether to raise these issues with Molitor at his deposition.

Singley asked to be paid for the work midway through Singley's research on the report. Counsel asked that Singley "hold off" till after they could seek a settlement.

When attempts at settlement failed, the expert again asked to be paid, before agreeing to appear at the deposition. Again, counsel asked if that payment could be delayed till after trial. Singley asked if a contingent fee arrangement could be entered into, whereby payment would be one-third of the total value of any settlement. The attorney instead suggested that in addition to the $20,000 in fees already incurred, the attorney would pay a bonus of $20,000 if the settlement was in access of $100,000 (to compensate the expert for the deposition testimony).

Expert Report of Dr. Sam F. Singley

Yount v. Molitor Management Group
Determination of Appropriate Discount

Section One
An Evaluation of the Value of Stocks In the Severance Agreement

1.0 Description of Engagement

Rowan & Rowan, LLP (the "Firm") was retained by attorney Pat Morgan of Mallory and Morgan to determine the appropriate discount for lack of marketability to be applied to certain stock certificates, specifically the 192,030 shares in TelexGlobalCorp ("TGLC") (the "Interest") pledged to Mr. Stephen F. Yount in the Severance Agreement dated April 30, YR-5, and amended October 6, YR-4.

1.1 Purpose and Use of the Report

The objective of this Report is to provide an opinion on the applicable discount for the Interest. This opinion is intended solely for the purpose outlined herein and should not be used for any other purpose. Our findings are not to be disclosed to other parties in connection with any other matters without first obtaining the expressed written authorization of the Managing Partner of Rowan & Rowan, LLP.

1.2 Sources of Information

Specific sources of information used in the development of this Report are outlined in Exhibit A.

1.3 Conclusion on Discount

Based on the Firm's analyses and considering all the relevant factors, it is our opinion that the appropriate discount is **forty percent.**

1.4 Significant Assumptions and Limiting Conditions

This Report and the conclusions reached herein are subject to certain "Limiting Conditions" as outlined in Exhibit B. Additionally, numerous assumptions were made during the performance of this Report and have been summarized in the Report. Readers are advised to read the entire Report and review all exhibits to fully understand all assumptions made.

1.5 Qualifications

Dr. Sam F. Singley, CPA/ABV, CFE, prepared this Report. Curriculum Vitae of the respective individual is attached in Exhibit C.

Section Two
Summary of Facts

2.0 Complaint and Background Information

The plaintiff in this matter is Stephen F. Yount, a former employee of Molitor Management Group, Inc. (MMG), a Nita corporation with offices located at 24 Yardley Executive Park, Yardley, Nita. Mr. Yount negotiated a severance package with Harold A. Molitor, the Chairman of MMG.

On April 30, YR-5, a Severance Agreement was entered into by and between Stephen F. Yount, Molitor Management Group, Inc., and Harold A. Molitor, individually (the Agreement). The Agreement stated the following:

> [i]n lieu of $7,212.00 owed to Stephen F. Yount (SFY) by Molitor Management Group, Inc., (MMG) SFY will purchase from MMG and Harold A. Molitor for set amount the following interest.

The securities identified in the letter were as follows:

Company	Interest
Insured Communications, Inc.	12.5% of the Molitor Management Group, Inc. (MMG) interest after deducting Molitor Technology's Fund 20 Sharing agreement
Roucher Central / Roucher Motors	12.5% of MMG's interest after deducting Molitor Technology's Fund 20 Sharing agreement
Engineous Software, Inc.	187 shares held by MMG
Nevada SoftwareTechnology Applications, Inc.	12,500 shares of Harold A. Molitor's interest
TelPower Corporation	12.5% of MMG's interest
TMS	10% of MMG's interest
TelexGlobalCorporation	192,030 shares held by MMG
The Technology Group, Inc.	1,613 warrants held by MMG

It is our understanding that none of the securities listed in the Agreement were ever transferred by Molitor Management Group, Inc., or Harold Molitor to Stephen F. Yount by May 31, YR-5, as agreed to in the April 30, YR-5, Severance Agreement.

On October 6, YR-4, MMG amended the Severance Agreement as follows:

> The original May 31, YR-5, date, by which Harold Molitor was obligated to cause certain enumerated interests to be transferred to SFY has extended to January 31, YR-3. Harold Molitor will cause these enumerated interests to be transferred to SFY on or before January 31, YR-3. To the extent Harold Molitor or MMG do not yet have possession or control of these interests as of the date for transfer, Harold Molitor will cause those interests, or any remaining portion thereof, to be transferred to SFY within ten days of receipt by him or by MMG. All other terms of the Severance Agreement shall remain unchanged.

One of the securities to be transferred was TelexGlobal Corporation (TGLC). TelexGlobal Corporation, formerly known as EHI, Inc. (EHI), was incorporated under the laws of the State of Delaware in July YR-11. Until May YR-7, EHI operated as a mall-based specialty retailer. In May YR-7, EHI sold substantially all of its assets to Earth Happening, Inc., for cash in the amount of $517,795 plus the assumption by Earth Happening, Inc., of specified liabilities. The completion of this sale terminated the active operations, and for the period May YR-7 through February 3, YR-5, EHI sought to serve as a vehicle to effect an acquisition, whether by merger, exchange of capital stock, acquisition of assets, or other similar business combination.

In February YR-5, EHI acquired the outstanding capital stock of Huba Hub Link Corporation, a privately held company organized under the laws of the Province of Ontario, Canada. Huba Hub Link Corporation was engaged in the business of providing telemarketing services to business clients. EHI acquired all the outstanding capital stock of Huba Hub Link Corporation from the shareholders in exchange for an aggregate of 13,011,339 shares of EHI common stock. As a result of this transaction, Huba Hub Link Corporation became a branch or operating entity of the EHI. In connection with the transaction, EHI changed its corporate name to TelexGlobal Corporation (referred to in the Report as TGLC).

The TGLC stock certificates that were to be transferred to Mr. Yount contained a restrictive legend. The legend indicates that the securities may not be resold in the marketplace unless they are registered with the SEC or are exempt from the registration requirements. Although restricted shares cannot be sold on the open market (a public stock exchange), shares may be sold in private transactions.

Had Mr. Yount received the stock in a timely fashion and been able to remove the restrictive legend, contribute to an exchange fund, met the United States Securities and Exchange Commission (SEC) requirement or sold the stock in a private transaction, he could have realized substantial value.

Below is a stock chart taken from 10Kwizard.com that details the stock price for TGLC for the last five years.

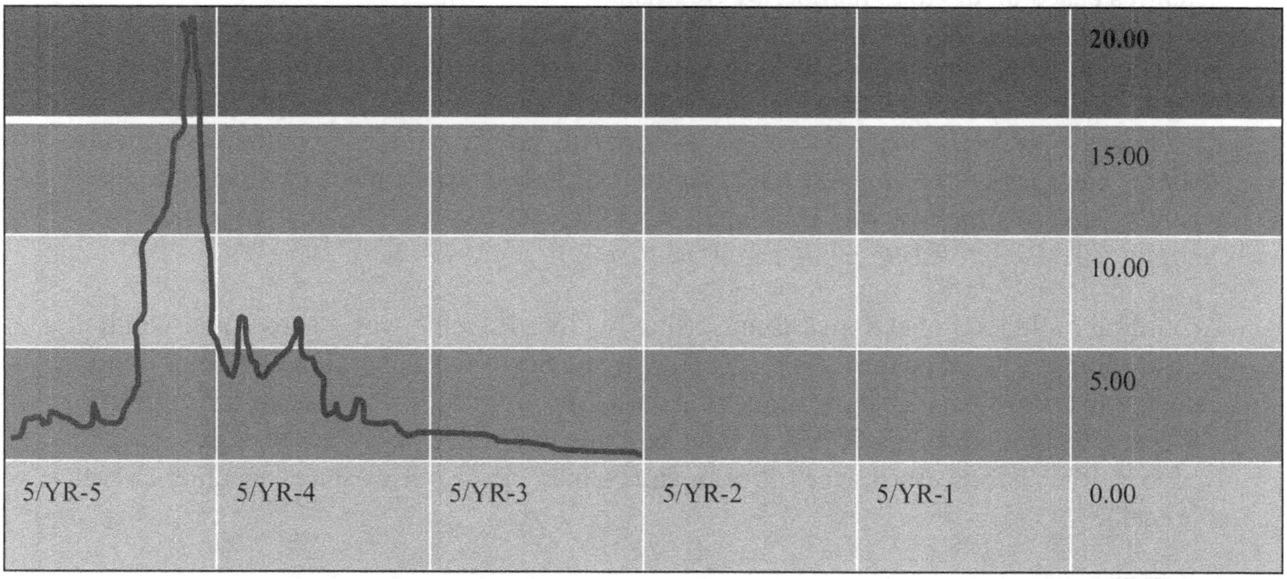

Had the stock certificates been transferred, Mr. Yount could have sold the stock either in the open market, if the restrictions were removed, or sold the stock in a private transaction at a discounted price. However, the opportunity to realize any substantial value has passed. In a press release from the Office of the New York State Attorney General Elliot Nesser (NYAGO), TGLC was indicted in a telemarketing scam described below:

> In a decision issued Thursday, the Third Department of the Supreme Court, Appellate Division affirmed a lower court decision against a Delaware corporation operating an advance-free credit card telemarketing scam out of Canada. The decision upheld an October YR-3 ruling by Justice Joseph C. Sacosi of Albany County State Supreme Court, which had halted the scam and awarded restitution to victimized consumers.
>
> "Yesterday's appellate ruling affirms my office's authority to protect the interests of individuals across the nation doing business with New York-based companies," Nesser said. "The ruling underscores the vital importance of maintaining the integrity of the marketplace in New York State."
>
> Using the name Simply Gold Benefits, TelexGlobal, Inc.'s, telemarketers promised thousands of consumers across the nation that for an advance fee of over $200, the consumers would receive a low-rate, general-purpose Visa or MasterCard credit card. In fact, consumers who paid the advance fee did not receive a credit card. Instead, TelexGlobal sent them a "discount benefits package" consisting of generally worthless items such as an application or a credit card.
>
> As part of its scheme, TelexGlobal used a "drop box" address in Champlain, New York, to send and receive mail to conceal the fact that its telemarketing operations were based in Canada.
>
> The lower court ruling banned further operation of the scam and ordered TelexGlobal to make full restitution to all consumers who made payments to the company, plus civil penalties based on the total number of victims.
>
> On appeal, TelexGlobal argued that the Attorney General could not obtain civil penalties or restitution for victims not located in New York State. In its decision, the Appellate Division held that the Attorney General has the authority to obtain relief for victims nationwide, stating, "New York has a vital interest in securing an honest marketplace in which to transact business, and this interest was threatened when TelexGlobal used a New York address to complete the deceptive transactions at issue here."
>
> According to TelexGlobal's own filings, Simply Gold Benefits was a substantial windfall for the company. In its quarterly report filed with the Securities and Exchange Commission, TelexGlobal reported that its revenues increased by over $8 million from $1 million in YR-5 to over $9.2 million in YR-4, in large part due to Simply Gold Benefits sales. To date, Nesser's office has received over 150 complaints, many from out-of-state consumers, about this scam.[1]

---

1. Office of the Nita Attorney General Elliot Nesser, May YR-2, http://bit.ly/1mAj3ec.

Although the stock price was sliding prior to the charges filed, the announcement of the lawsuits effectively eliminated the market value of TGLC. In the last year, the TGLC had few transactions and those that did occur were at substantially reduced values, as indicated in the chart below for the period May YR-3 to May YR-2.

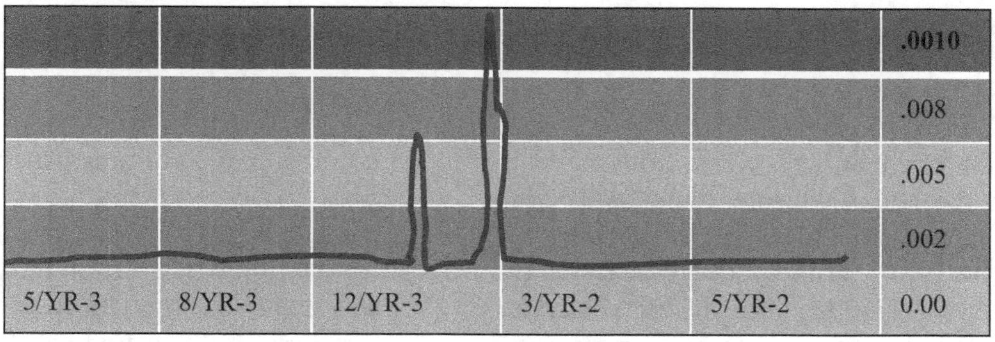

Section Three
Valuation Conclusion

3.0 Common Adjustments to Value

To determine the fair market value of the Interest, the Firm generally considered a number of adjustments to the preliminary valuation conclusions before arriving at the final valuation conclusion. A common adjustment is a discount associated with the liquidity, or pace of marketability, of the Interest being valued.

The following quote describes these adjustments best:

> In their arguments, neither petitioner nor respondent clearly focuses on the fact that two conceptually distinct discounts are involved here, one for lack of marketability and the other for lack of control. The minority shareholder discount is designed to reflect the decreased value of shares that do not convey control of a closely held corporation. The lack of marketability (or illiquidity) discount, on the other hand, is designed to reflect the fact that there is no ready market for shares in a closely held corporation. Although there may be some overlap between these two discounts in that lack of control may reduce marketability, it should be borne in mind that even controlling shares in a nonpublic corporation suffer from lack of marketability because of the absence of a ready private placement market and the fact that flotation costs would have to be incurred if the corporation were to publicly offer its stock.[2]

3.1 Discount for Lack of Marketability

An ownership interest in an entity has a greater value if it is readily marketable and easily converted to cash. An interest that is not readily marketable is less desirable, and thus there is less demand for that interest. The impact of a lack of marketability on the market value of financial assets has been analyzed and discussed in business texts and periodicals. There have been several studies conducted

2. Estate of Andrews v. Comm'r, 79 T.C. 938 (1982).

that attempt to quantify the impact of the respective discount. These studies fall into one of two basic categories, depending on the type of market transaction data on which they are predicted upon:

1. Studies of transactions in closely held stocks prior to initial public offerings.

2. Restricted ("letter") stock studies.

3.2 Pre-IPO Studies

Restricted stocks are only restricted from public trading for a limited period of time. After this period has elapsed, the stocks can enter the market.

A study performed by Emory Business Valuation LLC (formerly known as the studies performed by an investment banking firm, Robert W. Baird & Co.) has attempted to quantify the difference in discount for closely held stock over restricted stock. A summary of the finding can be found in Shannon Pratt's monthly newsletter, *Business Valuation Update*, or in the text entitled *Business Valuation Discounts and Premiums*, by Shannon P. Pratt. Emory analyzed initial public offerings to determine the relationship between the price at which the stock was initially offered to the public and the price at which private sales were transacted prior to the initial public offering. The results of this study were that the private buyers paid, on average, approximately forty to forty-five percent less than the price at which the stock subsequently came to market.

Another set of studies, referred to as the Pre-IPO studies, focused on private transactions prior to public offerings. They were intended to reflect the higher discounts of closely held stock relative to restricted shares that typically could be sold in the public market after some period of time. The studies utilized data from registration statements required to be filed with the SEC when companies sell securities to the public. The results of this study were that the private buyers paid, on average, approximately forty to forty-five percent less than the price at which the stock subsequently came to market.

Willamette Management Associates also produced several studies that detailed the average discount for lack of marketability. According to Shannon Pratt, this series of studies was initially conducted to assist in quantifying the discount for lack of marketability in the *Estate of Gallo v. Commissioner*.[3] Willamette compared the private transaction price with the price the shares were offered at as of the initial public offering date. Certain adjustments are necessary to compensate for differences in earnings as to the transaction date and the offering date. This process is described in detail in Shannon Pratt's *Business Valuation Discounts and Premiums*. The analysis conducted by Willamette has been prepared for numerous time periods ranging from YR-29 to YR-7.

Pratt goes on to state:

> Because of the very high cost of these detailed studies, Willamette has not published the complete lists of stocks involved in each year's study. Willamette publishes a summary of the studies but not the underlying data. The relevant data have, however, been provided to courts and opposing experts under a confidentiality agreement in many cases involving

3. Estate of Gallo v. Comm'r, T.C. Memo 1985-363, T.C.M. (CCH) 470 (1985).

disputed discounts for lack of marketability so that opposing experts could conduct effective cross-examinations.[4]

Valuation Advisors analyzed 679 transactions of common stock and options of 336 companies prior to successfully completing their initial public offering in YR-5. Using the data for transactions within two years of initial public offering, the firm found the average discount to be 48.97 percent. The study also provided further evidence that as the length of time to liquidity increases, the respective discount for lack of marketability increases. In simple terms, the longer the anticipated holding period is, the greater the discount. Below is a table dealing with the days prior to the initial public offering and the average discount witnessed.[5]

Days Before IPO	Average Discount (%)	Number of Transactions
1–90	32.45	166
91–180	52.06	163
181–270	65.84	99
271–365	73.69	84
366–730	77.19	167

The reader should note that the study examined a number of companies considered to be "new economy" companies.[6] Many stock had little to no earning at the time of the initial public offering, and over half of the companies were less than five years old.

3.3 Discount for Lack of Marketability Chosen

To determine the reduction in value the market would demand from this investment, we identified 341 transactions we considered similar to this investment from a financial perspective. To identify the respective transactions, we relied on the Valuation Advisors' Lack of Marketability Discount Study (VALMD Study). This database was developed by Brain Pearson of Valuation Advisors, LLC, and compares the initial public offering (IPO) stock price to pre-IPO common stock, common stock option, and convertible preferred stock prices. These market-based transactions demonstrate the lack of marketability discount afforded by the pre-IPO instruments because of their illiquidity when issued by a privately held company. The study includes pre-IPO transactions from 1995 to present. Using the following criteria, we identified 342 guideline companies to use to determine the discount:

1. Revenues
2. Operating Income
3. Common stock transactions only

4. Shannon P. Pratt, *Business Valuation Discounts and Premiums* (YR-3), at 84.
5. *Id.* at 87.
6. *Id.*

Our search criteria were as follows:

Criteria	Subject Company	VALMD Range
Revenues	QE7/29/YR-4 Revenues were $4,959,701	<$100,000,000
Operating Income	QE7/29/YR-4 ($1,919,970)	<=0
Number of Companies Identified		341

From this search, we identified 341 transactions for 253 separate companies in various industries. The average discount negotiated depended on the period of time between the IPO and the transaction. Since we are dealing with restricted stock that has a market place already established, we focused on transactions within twelve months of the initial public offering. Below is a table detailing the results of our search:

Months Prior to IPO	Average Discount (%)
0	31.27
1	28.39
2	30.39
3	28.00
4	35.54
5	50.53
6	41.64
7	44.83
8	62.22
9	58.63
10	72.08
11	49.77
12	63.63

The average discount ranged between twenty-eight percent and approximately seventy-two percent, depending on the holding period.

We believe it would be somewhat difficult to sell the Interest and would require time and money to complete a sale. However, since restricted stocks, by definition, are stocks for companies that already have an established market, the discount should be lower than the discounts witnessed for private companies preparing for an IPO. Based on the above data, and on our knowledge of the market as well as the financial performance of TGLC compared to that of entities in similar financial condition, a discount of forty percent from the freely traded price appears reasonable. We believe that such a discount would be sufficient to induce a buyer to invest in the securities and still provide a reasonable return to the seller. This conclusion is at the high end for the Restricted Stock studies and around the average for Pre-IPO studies.

This implies a value as follows:

		TGLC	
		6/1/YR-5	1/31/YR-3
Number of Shares Held		192,030.00	192,030.00
Price Per Share		$ 0,8750	$ 1,8125
Total Value (Unrestricted)		$ 168,026.25	$ 348,054.38
Applicable Discount	40%	$ (67,210.50)	$ (139,221.75)
Value (Restricted)		$ 100,815.75	$ 208,832.63

June 1, YR-5, was used since the stock was not traded on May 31, YR-5.

3.4 A Second Approach—Restricted (Letter) Stock Studies

TelexGlobal Corporation is a public corporation trading on the securities markets. Unlike many issues of stock, its value is based on the value of its recent acquisition of a private company and its subsequent reformulation as a new company operating a new business. The Plaintiff's Interest was subject to a restrictive legend that limited its marketability in these circumstances. The Plaintiff could only sell the Interest on the open market if he was able to remove the restriction in a timely manner. If he was unable to remove the restrictions, he could sell his shares on the private market. This lack of marketability limits the Interest's value. This was succinctly articulated by William Silber, who stated:

Companies issuing restricted stock alongside registered securities trading in the open market usually offer a price discount on the restricted securities to compensate for their relative illiquidity.

This part of the report analyzes restricted stock studies to determine the fair market value of the Plaintiff's Interest. These studies compare the prices of restricted stock sales to the freely traded stock price on the same day. Restricted stock studies are the most widely used tool to determine discounts for lack of marketability and are the studies most often accepted by the Tax Courts.[7] It is believed that since the shares are identical in every respect except for trading status, the difference is due solely to liquidity issues. Below is a summary of the Restricted Stock Studies frequently cited and the average (or median) discount realized.

7. Espen Robak and Lance S. Hal, "Bringing Sanity to Marketability Discounts: A New Data Source," available at http://people.stern.nyu.edu/adamodar/pdfiles/eqnotes/fmvstudyarticle.pdf.

Study	Time Period of Study	Discount (%)
SEC Overall	1966–69	25.8
SEC nonreporting OTC Companies	1966–69	32.6
Gelman Study	1968–70	33.0
Trout Study	1968–72	33.5
Moroney Study	1972–73	35.6
Maher Study	1968–73	35.4
Standard Research Consultants Study	1978–82	45.0
Willamette Management Associates Study	1981–84	31.2
Silber Study	1981–89	33.8
FMV Study	1979–93	23.0
FMV Restricted Stock Study	1980–87	22.3
Management Planning, Inc.	1980–96	27.1
Bruce Johnson	1991–95	20.0
Columbia Financial Advisors	1996–97	21.0
Columbia Financial Advisors	1997–98	13.0

The various studies examine hundreds of transactions over a significant period of time. Discounts typically ranged between thirty and thirty-five percent; after 1990, however, when the SEC relaxed the restrictions on restricted stock, the discounts dropped. This is especially true for transactions subsequent to YR-8, when the SEC reduced the holding period from two years to only one year. This drop is consistent with our belief that one of the primary factors in the discount determination is the required holding period.

One of the most widely cited studies on this matter, by Michael Hertzel and Richard Smith, comes to a different conclusion than the weight of academic material. The study by Hertzel and Smith has been cited for the proposition that the discount associated with decreased liquidity is closer to 13.5 percent. Due to the lack of transparency in these studies, combined with the studies' small sample sizes, no study has been treated as conclusive.[8]

3.5 Applying Restricted Stock Studies to the Plaintiff's Interest

The plaintiff's Interest in THCL was established by contract in YR-5 and amended in YR-4. This obligation involved equity after YR-13, after the SEC relaxed restrictions on restricted stock. Thus, this report determines the fair market value of the Interest using the average discount rate for three studies initiated and completed in the 1990s.

8. Espen Robak and Lance S. Hal, "Bringing Sanity to Marketability Discounts: A New Data Source," available at http://people.stern.nyu.edu/adamodar/pdfiles/eqnotes/fmvstudyarticle.pdf (stating that "[t]he studies listed above were mostly performed on small samples of restricted stock transactions. Also, most of the studies listed in the table provide little or no detail about how the discount varies around the average." This quote referred to several studies that are included in the chart above.

Bruce Johnson	YR-15–YR-10	20.0%
Columbia Financial Advisors	YR-9–YR-8	21.0%
Columbia Financial Advisors	YR-8–YR-7	13.0%
Average		18.0%

The average discount rate for these three studies is 18.0 percent. Given this discount rate, the value of the Plaintiff's Interest is:

		TGLC	
		1/31/YR-3	6/1/YR-5
Number of Shares Held		192,030.00	192,030.00
Price Per Share		$ 1,8750	$ 1,8125
Total Value (Unrestricted)		$ 168,026.25	$ 348,054.38
Applicable Discount	18%	$ (30,244.73)	$ (62,649.79)
Value (Restricted)		$ 137,781.52	$ 285,404.59

3.6 Valuation Conclusion

In the Summary, we offer two values for the restricted shares of TGLC during the period 6/1/YR-5 and 1/31/YR-3. Under the first method, the value is between $100,815.75 and $208,832.63 (average of $154,824.19); under the second method, the value is between $137,781.52 and $285,404.59 (average of $211,592.55). Weighting these methods equally yields an average valuation for TGLC of $183,208.37

I have also been asked to opine on the value of a second stock, standard tech. I valued that stock according the valuation given by its owner, Harold Molitor, in statements he made to his investors. These statements represent the best estimate of its value during the period of time in question, end of YR-4 to the beginning of YR-3.

According to the letter dated January 17, YR-3, prepared by Molitor Technology Management Group and signed by Harold Molitor as Portfolio Manager and President, Standard TECH was believed to have a value of $12.50 per share while implying a value of $156,250 in addition to the value of the TelexGlobal Stock. We have considered this the best indication of value; it is evidenced in writing to shareholders and discusses the outlook of the entity.

Total $183.208.37 + $156,250.00 = $339,458.37

Supplementary Response to Connors's Opinion

Connors's opinion is based on two assumptions: 1) that there was no value for TGLC stock during this time, and 2) that Harold Molitor's statements were material misrepresentations and should not be taken as factual. With regard to the value of TGLC, Molitor himself believed otherwise as evidence by his purchase of the restricted stock during YR-4 and his representation in his newsletter that the stock value had risen from its December 31, YR-4, value of $1-11/16 a share to $2.91 a share. In addition, the studies I cite include companies with all the attributes that Connors is looking for. None of the studies suggests these shares have no value at all. In addition, 10Kwizard.com provided daily quotes for the price of TGLC during the entire period, indicating there was value in the market of its unrestricted stock. Therefore, valuation methods in relationship to trades in unrestricted stock are the best indication of its market value at the time. Of note is the fact that one of the studies I rely on was conducted by Connors's own firm.

Section Four
Certification of Value (USPAP Standards Rule 10-3)

We certify that, to the best of my knowledge and belief:

- The statements of fact contained in this report are true and correct.
- The reported analyses, opinions, and conclusions are limited only by the reported assumptions and limiting conditions, and are my personal, impartial, and unbiased professional analyses, opinions, and conclusions.
- We have no present or prospective interest in the property that is the subject of this report and no personal interest with respect to the parties involved.
- We have no bias with respect to the property that is the subject of this report or to the parties involved with this assignment.
- Our engagement in this assignment was not contingent upon developing or reporting predetermined results.
- Our compensation for the completing this assignment is not contingent upon the development or reporting of a predetermined value or direction in value that favors the cause of the client, the amount of the value opinion, the attainment of a stipulated result, or the occurrence of a subsequent event directly related to the intended use of this appraisal.
- Our analyses, opinions, and conclusions were developed, and this report has been prepared, in conformity with the Uniform Standards of Professional Appraisal Practice.
- No one provided significant business valuation appraisal assistance to the individuals signing this certification.

ROWAN & ROWAN, LLP

Sam F. Singley

Sam F. Singley,
CPA/ABV, CFE, Managing Partner

Exhibit A
Sources of Information

1. *Guide to Business Valuations*, Practitioners Publishing Company, June YR-1

2. *Valuing a Business: The Analysis and Appraisal of Closely Held Companies*, 4th edition, Shannon P. Pratt, Robert F. Reilly, Robert P. Schweihs, YR-4

3. *Business Valuation Discounts and Premiums*, Shannon P. Pratt, YR-3

4. The deposition of Stephen Yount, taken August 15, YR-1

5. The deposition of Harold Molitor, taken July 31, YR-1

6. The complaint Stephen F. Yount v. Molitor Management Group, Inc., and Harold A. Molitor, filed by Mallory and Morgan

7. TelexGlobal Corp. Form 10QSB for the quarter ended July 29, YR-4

8. Reuters Pro-Vestor Plus Company Report, TelexGlobalCorporation, May 12, YR-1

9. Molitor Technology Management Corp. letter dated January 17, YR-3, to the Molitor Technology Fund L.P. Investor

Exhibit B
Limiting Conditions

1. This Report was performed for the sole use identified in the engagement letter. This Report and any information contained within this Report are not to be used for any other purpose by any other party. Such other use will render the Report invalid and is not authorized. This Report and/or its finding are not to be included in, or referred to, in any offering memorandum (public or private) or prospectus of any kind.

2. The Firm assumes no responsibility for damages of any kind resulting from reliance on the Report.

3. The Report was based on historical and projected financial statements and other information supplied by Management. Certain adjustments, data, other information, and analyses in this Report were based on consideration of other information supplied by these parties, trade and professional associations, and other resources. While these parties are believed to be reliable, no representations or warranties are made as such. The Firm has not independently verified any of this data and expresses no opinion regarding its accuracy or reliability.

4. The Firm assumes no responsibility for matters of legal or tax-oriented nature affecting any of the property valued or any opinion of title. The Firm assumed that all property is readily transferable, free and clear of all liens and encumbrances of any kind, except as specifically stated within the Report. Certain assets of the Company may be secured by bank indebtedness and are subject to loan agreements with certain restrictive covenants and conditions. Readers of this Report should review the agreements with legal counsel to determine their full ramifications.

5. This Report is not to be used for any allocation of values for various individual assets or asset classes as may be required by the Internal Revenue Service or for any other tax-related purpose. No legal, tax, or accounting opinions were expressed within this report, nor is any opinion expressed as to the accuracy or validity of any of the financial information contained within this Report or its conformity with accounting principles generally accepted in the United States.

6. This Report assumes there are no factors such as restrictive agreements of any kind, other than those specifically noted within this Report, which would impair value in any way or the ability to affect an expedient sales of the ownership interest being valued.

7. Nothing in this Report constitutes a recommendation regarding the purchase or sale of any securities or assets. The Firm expresses no opinion, guarantee, or assurance of any kind, express or implied, in the potential investment performance resulting from a purchase of an interest in the Company.

8. The Firm assumed for the purpose of this engagement that the Company was in good standing and was not in violation of any laws or regulatory statues of any kind. The Firm has undertaken no procedures to independently verify these assumptions. This engagement assumes no

contingent or other liabilities of any kind (e.g., pending or threatening litigation, environmental or hazardous waste, or other similar matters.) These issues were outside the scope of this Report; however, if considered, could have a material impact on the final valuation.

9. This Report and its information and findings are confidential and are not to be published, copied, reproduced, disclosed, or disseminated in any way by any means, in whole or in part, without the express prior written permission of the Firm. This Report is copyrighted and remains the property of the Firm.

10. The Valuation Date is stated in the Report without any guarantees as to the final valuation conclusion at the Valuation Date or any future date, or any contrary opinions as the final valuation conclusion of the same date. The Firm shall be under no obligations to update this Report or its findings for any reason.

11. The Valuation Date to which the conclusion and opinions expressed in this Report is set forth herein. The final valuation conclusion reported is based on the purchasing power of the United States dollar as of that date. The Firm assumes no responsibility for economic or physical factors occurring subsequent to the date that may affect the opinions reported.

12. Hazardous substances, if present within a facility, can introduce an actual or potential liability that would adversely impact the marketability and value of the property being valued. Such liability may be in the form of immediate recognition of existing hazardous conditions. Future liability could stem from the release of non-hazardous contaminants such as asbestos fibers or toxic vapors from area formaldehyde foam insulation, through again or building renovations. In the development of the Firm's opinion, no consideration was given to such a liability or its impact on the final valuation conclusion.

13. The final valuation conclusion assumes a "going-concern" premise, based on an all-cash purchase or equivalent terms thereof. The Company would have a materially different value in liquidation. No estimate of the final valuation conclusion that could be achieved in liquidation is presented in this Report, unless stated otherwise.

14. All of the representations and information supplied by Management and their agents are assumed to true, accurate, and complete and have not been verified by the Firm in any way.

Exhibit C
Curriculum Vitae

Dr. Sam F. Singley
CPA/ABV, CFE, Managing Partner
Rowan & Rowan, LLP
90 Canal Street
Central, Nita 01514
(555) 227-4645

Current Position

Managing Partner and Partner in Charge of Management Advisory and Litigation Support Services Practice Group.

Professional History and Education

- Rowan & Rowan, LLP Partner, YR-5 - present
- Professor Emeritus, Nita State University, YR-5 - present
- McDonald Chaired Professor of Economics, Nita State University, YR-21 - YR-5
- Professor, Nita State University, YR-27 - YR-21
- Associate Professor, Nita State University, YR-30 - YR-27
- Assistant Professor, Nita State University, YR-35 - YR-30
- Teaching Fellow in Economics and Politics, Princeton University, YR-37 - YR-35
- PhD in Mathematics, Princeton University
- MS in Mathematics, University of Pennsylvania
- BS in Mathematical Economics, Gettysburg College

Practice Areas

General Client Services – Responsible for all phases of providing auditing, tax, and accounting services, including planning, staffing, and client communication.

Management Advisory and Litigation Support Services – Including litigation consulting, forensic accounting, fraud analysis, financial analysis, valuations, damage calculations, ability to pay analysis.

Court Appointments – Served as court appointed Receiver, Guardian, Conservator, Administrator, and Master.

Mergers and Acquisitions – Advisory including preparation of valuations, preparations of financing and business plans, acquisition structure, and negotiation.

General Management and Financial Consulting – Including cost and price analysis, financial reporting, compensation planning, financial planning, financing, and cash flow planning.

Recent Expert Testimony

Kendall v. Hyannis Restorations et al.	Trial	YR-1, YR-2, YR-3, YR-5	Nita
Cerundulo v. Cerundulo	Trial	YR-1	Nita
Friedman v. Friedman	Deposition and Trial	YR-1	Nita
Gersten v. Klasfeld	Deposition	YR-1	Florida
Keating v. Keating	Trial	YR-1	Nita
Krauledat v. Harvard Bioscience	Arbitration Testimony	YR-1	Nita
Zalis v. Gertsen	Deposition and Trial	YR-2	Florida
Brighton v. Lopez et al.	Deposition	YR-1	Nita
Katherine Robinson v. Price Waterhouse	Deposition and Trial	YR-1	Nita
Bonderman v. Bonderman	Trial	YR-5	Nita

Professional Memberships, Affiliations, and Accomplishments

- Certified Public Accountant Accredited in Business Valuation (ABV)
- Certified Fraud Examiner (CFE)
- Diplomat of the American Board of Forensic Accounting
- Editorial Advisor to Breaking into Litigation Support for CPAs
- Nita Society of Certified Public Accountants
- American Institute of Certified Public Accountants
- Member of a team of U.S. Accounting Professionals touring throughout People's Republic of China; lectured Chinese officials, educators, and business people on U.S. system of accounting, taxation, and joint venture structure
- Designed and launched Innovative Accounting Program for Nita State University Past Member of the Advisory Board of CPA Profit Report
- Who's Who Among Rising Americans
- Speaker at AICPA National Conference on forensic accounting Washington, D.C.
- Speaker to MSCPA meeting on litigation consulting and forensic accounting
- Speaker to National Conference of CPA's concerning mergers and acquisitions and management advisory services
- Guest lecturer, Northeastern University and Central University graduate schools regarding new ventures and valuations
- Speaker to many associations, banks, insurance companies, and law firms on various business, tax, and litigation issues
- Speaker to the Central Estate Planning Council and the International Association of Financial Planners on valuation issues of closely held businesses
- Quoted in *The Wall Street Journal*, *American Banker*, *Family Business Magazine*, *New Business Magazine*, *CFO Magazine*, *Boston Globe*, *Central Business Journal*

- Interviewed on The Wall Street Journal Radio Network and WCVB Business News segment
- Contributing author to *Income Reconstruction: A Guide to Discovering Unreported Income*, published by American Institute of Certified Public Accountants
- Articles in *Lawyer's Weekly, Litigation Service Counselor, Hanover Report, Your Company, The CPA Management Consultant, Central Business Journal, Mass High Tech Weekly*

Community Service/Appointments

Member, Judicial Nominating Commission

Board Member, Courageous Sailing Center

Finance Director, Campaign Committee for District Attorney

Financial Consultant to various campaign committees

Summary of Deposition of Defendant's Expert—Jamie R. Connors

Went through credentials. Has done litigation support since early in his career with Deloitte. Left academia as an assistant professor at University of Chicago because saw the business opportunities in providing expert testimony. It was a good move. Connors was made a director at Deloitte in four years, making over $1 million dollars a year since that time.

Employed by attorney for Molitor. Molitor suggested Connors to counsel because they knew each other since Furman. After Furman, Connors went and played minor league baseball for the Richmond Braves (an Atlanta Braves affiliate) for five years. He then coached high school baseball before going back to Nita State to get a PhD in economics. He and Molitor had remained friends over the years, had gone to ball games together, and commiserated together when each divorced. Connors learned about the case while visiting Molitor last year and became intrigued by it because of the subject matter. He offered to get involved at a reduced rate to help out his friend.

Expert has dealt with a number of different stock valuation matters involving stocks that have limited or no actual market, but where a hypothetical market might be created as a substitute means to determine the value of the restricted stock. Feels that at best it was the value of the travel expenses Molitor promised to reimburse, or about $7,000. Connors doesn't think there is enough reliable data to be able to create a hypothetical market for these stocks. Because he wants to limit his time commitments in the case, he wonders if he could simply spend his time reacting to the plaintiff's expert report. That way he could use statistical tools to attack the plaintiff's report and opine that it is based on insufficient data. He has done this for many defendants over the years and has been successful in supporting *Daubert* motions (had the effect of throwing out plaintiff's expert opinions and ending their cases). He confides that such opinions can be justified (not sufficient data to know value) in almost every case that he has been involved in.

Expert was given a copy of the contract between the parties and reviewed it. He is familiar with the contract between the parties and its extension. He has reviewed the depositions of both parties.

Expert was employed by attorney for Molitor after the case was filed and didn't start work till after Singley's opinion was submitted.

Expert talked with Molitor's attorney directly about his understanding of the value of the stock that was listed in the agreement. Attorney asked expert to assume, but only for the purposes of this report, that Molitor was legally bound to turn over TelexGlobal restricted stock during the time of October YR-4 to January 31, YR-3. Further, counsel asked expert to assume that TelexGlobal had been operating fraudulently in its business practices during the time Molitor was bound to turn over the stock to Yount.

Attorney showed the expert the NY AG's press release concerning TelexGlobal, and the expert was told that the release occurred shortly after the time designated in the agreement for the stock to have been delivered to Yount. Expert verified this by checking the dates in the agreement and of the release.

Expert did consult stock trades of TelexGlobal restricted stock in the months preceding the AG press release. He didn't find any record of any actual trades that occurred during that time. He does not think that 10Kwizard changes its pricing based on actual sales, only on bid and ask prices.

[*Authors' Note: The following are interview notes only and are meant to raise a number of issues for discussion of ethical issues in working with experts.*]

Expert confided that he was bothered by the existence of the 10Kwizard and its quotes during this time. He was also curious as to how Molitor got the stock in the first place. He was worried about how he could explain why Molitor had paid what he had paid for the stock, and also why his newsletter indicated such an aggressive value for the stock during this time. He could only imagine his friend was speculating and hoping to "put one over" on his own partners.

Expert never reviewed any publicly available financial information on TelexGlobal or Nevada Software Standard TECH because he told counsel that while it might reveal something relevant about the value of these stocks and it would be something he normally did, it wouldn't be worth his time, especially since Singley hadn't bothered to do this.

In the expert's first draft of his report, he made the following statements.

"While valuing restricted stock is often quite speculative, that is not to say that there are no times when there is value in such stock. Often, family, friends, and community investors are willing to buy such stock in an attempt to get in on what they see is an important business opportunity."

That sentence has been deleted from his final report because it was poorly written and contains a double negative.

Connors revealed that the language he used in the draft was taken from an earlier expert report he rendered in another case. That case was *Benfield v. Boston Securities Traders Organization* and is listed on his résumé. In that case, he had opined that the defendant was right to place value on restricted stock held in its own account and that it was selling to its clients. At the time he gave that opinion, he had not conducted any research into the market for restricted stock. He doesn't know whether his report or testimony was ever made public. He doubts it, as he thinks it was settled and subject to a confidentiality order.

Connors asked counsel what he should do about the fact that Molitor told him he knew the GlobalTech management very well. This statement may indicate that he may have been privy to their fraud and that they were paying him to help them unload their stock. Molitor told him he tried to unload it, but that there were no takers for stock.

Expert Report of Dr. Jamie R. Connors

(Expert for the Defendant, Harold Molitor and MMG, Inc.)

Valuation of the Restricted Stock
During the Period of June 1, YR-5, to January 31, YR-3

The purpose of this report is to evaluate, based on reasonable economic probabilities, the value of TelexGlobal restricted stock during the period of June 1, YR-5, to January 31, YR-3. I was asked to assume that the stock was transferred to Mr. Stephen (Fred) Yount. While I do not believe was validly transferred to Mr. Yount, I express no opinion on this transfer, but assume that it was a legal transfer. My opinion is that the value of such restricted stock is unknowable.

I have also been asked to opine on the value of the Standard TECH stock during this period of time. I place no value on Mr. Molitor's own statement's concerning it value. The fact that within a year it had no value suggests his statements were forward-looking statements and not meant to be relied on.

Value of TelexGlobal

I start with Dr. Sam Singley's findings of fact concerning the nature of TelexGlobal and have bolded his opinions that I find objectionable.

On October 6, YR-4, MMG amended the Severance Agreement as follows:

> The original May 31, YR-5, date, by which Harold Molitor was obligated to cause certain enumerated interests to be transferred to SFY has extended to January 31, YR-3. Harold Molitor will cause these enumerated interests to be transferred to SFY on or before January 31, YR-3. To the extent Harold Molitor or MMG do not yet have possession or control of these interests as of the date for transfer, Harold Molitor will cause those interests, or any remaining portion thereof, to be transferred to SFY within ten days of receipt by him or by MMG. All other terms of the Severance Agreement shall remain unchanged.

One of the securities to be transferred was TelexGlobal Corporation (TGLC). TelexGlobal Corporation, formerly known as EHI, Inc. (EHI), was incorporated under the laws of the State of Delaware in July YR-11. Until May YR-7, EHI operated as a mall-based specialty retailer. In May YR-7, EHI sold substantially all of its assets to Earth Happening, Inc. for cash in the amount of $517,795 plus the assumption by Earth Happening, Inc. of specified liabilities. The completion of this sale terminated the active operations, and for the period May YR-7 through February 3, YR-5, EHI sought to serve as a vehicle to effect an acquisition, whether by merger, exchange of capital stock, acquisition of assets, or other similar business combination.

In February YR-5, EHI acquired the outstanding capital stock of Huba Hub Link Corporation, a privately held company organized under the laws of the Province of Ontario, Canada. Huba Hub Link Corporation was engaged in the business of providing telemarketing services to business clients. EHI acquired all the outstanding capital stock of Huba Hub Link Corporation from the shareholders in exchange for an aggregate of 13,011,339 shares of EHI common stock. As a result of this transaction, Huba Hub Link Corporation became a branch or operating entity of the EHI. In connection with the transaction, EHI changed its corporate name to TelexGlobal Corporation (referred to in the Report as TGLC).

The TGLC stock certificates that were to be transferred to Mr. Yount contained a restrictive legend. The legend indicates that the securities may not be resold in the marketplace unless they are registered with the SEC or are exempt from the registration requirements. **Although restricted shares cannot be sold on the open market (a public stock exchange), shares may be sold in private transactions.**

Had Mr. Yount received the stock in a timely fashion and been able to remove the restrictive legend, contribute to an exchange fund, met the United States Securities and Exchange Commission (SEC) requirement or sold the stock in a private transaction, he could have realized substantial value.

Below is a stock chart taken from 10Kwizard.com that details the stock price for TGLC for the last five years.

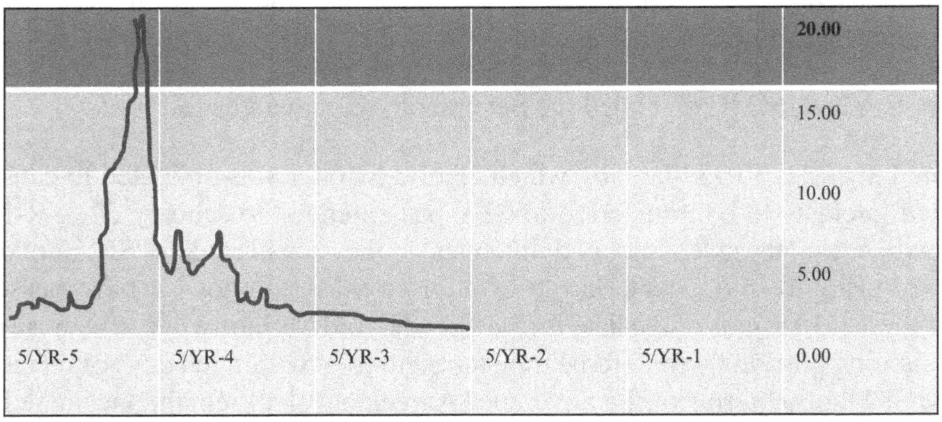

Had the stock certificates been transferred, Mr. Yount could have sold the stock either in the open market, if the restrictions were removed, or sold the stock in a private transaction at a discounted price. However, the opportunity to realize any substantial value has passed. In a press release from the Office of the New York State Attorney General Elliot Nesser (NYAGO), TGLC was indicted in a telemarketing scam described below:

> In a decision issued Thursday, the Third Department of the Supreme Court, Appellate Division affirmed a lower court decision against a Delaware corporation operating an advance-free

credit card telemarketing scam out of Canada. The decision upheld an October YR-3 ruling by Justice Joseph C. Sacosi of Albany County State Supreme Court, which had halted the scam and awarded restitution to victimized consumers.

Yesterday's appellate ruling affirms my office's authority to protect the interests of individuals across the nation doing business with New York-based companies," Nesser said. "The ruling underscores the vital importance of maintaining the integrity of the marketplace in New York State."

Using the name Simply Gold Benefits, TelexGlobal, Inc.'s, telemarketers promised thousands of consumers across the nation that for an advance fee of over $200, the consumers would receive a low-rate, general-purpose Visa or MasterCard credit card. In fact, consumers who paid the advance fee did not receive a credit card. Instead, TelexGlobal sent them a "discount benefits package" consisting of generally worthless items such as an application or a credit card.

As part of its scheme, TelexGlobal used a "drop box" address in Champlain, New York, to send and receive mail to conceal the fact that its telemarketing operations were based in Canada.

The lower court ruling banned further operation of the scam and ordered TelexGlobal to make full restitution to all consumers who made payments to the company, plus civil penalties based on the total number of victims.

On appeal, TelexGlobal argued that the Attorney General could not obtain civil penalties or restitution for victims not located in New York State. In its decision, the Appellate Division held that the Attorney General has the authority to obtain relief for victims nationwide, stating, "New York has a vital interest in securing an honest marketplace in which to transact business, and this interest was threatened when TelexGlobal used a New York address to complete the deceptive transactions at issue here."

According to TelexGlobal's own filings, Simply Gold Benefits was a substantial windfall for the company. In its quarterly report filed with the Securities and Exchange Commission, TelexGlobal reported that its revenues increased by over $8 million from $1 million in YR-5 to over $9.2 million in YR-4, in large part due to Simply Gold Benefits sales. To date, Nesser's office has received over 150 complaints, many from out-of-state consumers, about this scam."[9]

Although the stock price was sliding prior to the charges filed, the announcement of the lawsuits effectively eliminated the market value of TGLC. In the last year, the TGLC had few transactions, and those that did occur were at substantially reduced values, as indicated in the chart below for the period May YR-3 to May YR-2.

9. Office of the NITA Attorney General Elliot Nesser, May YR-2, http://bit.ly/1mAj3ec.

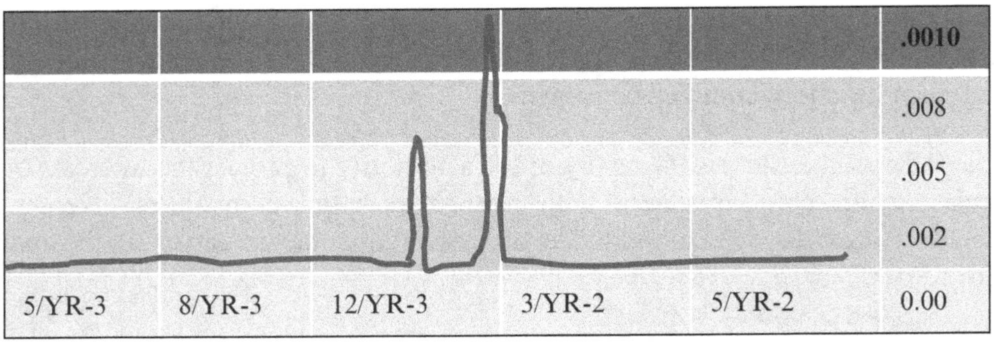

Problems with Dr. Singley's Opinions

I find from these statements a number of variables that need to be factored into any calculation of TGLC's value. One is the nature of the restriction on the stock at the time Mr. Molitor held it, and the second is the value in the market place of a stock whose value depended on illegal activity.

As an initial matter, Dr. Singley's own limitation to his valuation of TGLC makes his opinion not of value. He says in limitation 8:

> 8. The Firm assumed for the purpose of this engagement that the Company was in good standing and was not in violation of any laws or regulatory statues of any kind. The Firm has undertaken no procedures to independently verify these assumptions. This engagement assumes no contingent or other liabilities of any kind (e.g., pending or threatening litigation, environmental or hazardous waste, or other similar matters.) These issues were outside the scope of this Report; however, if considered, could have a material impact on the final valuation.

In addition, as to the first variable in Dr. Singley's calculation, there is nothing in the record that indicates the nature of the restriction on the TelexGlobal stock. Restrictions might be based on the fact that the stocks were registered to founders, officers, or directors subject to an IPO. On the other hand, the restrictions might be related to the company obtaining a certain profitability in their audited financial statements. Without knowing the nature of the restrictions to the sale of stock it is impossible to determine the value of the stock. For example, if Mr. Molitor had bought this stock in a private transaction from a TelexGlobal officer or director, he likely waived his ability to sue such director and officer. Purchases of restricted stock in private sales often carry no redress to the buyer if the stock turns out to have no value. TelexGlobal's restrictions are not likely to have been based on time, as we have an understanding the stock was issued in February of YR-5, but no indication of that the restriction was removed on February YR-4, the standard length of time for restrictions on sales to officers and directors. Since these restrictions are likely for one year, this type of restriction would drop by the passage of time.

The same is not true for restrictions based on the company later producing a profit at a certain level. These types of restrictions produce even less in the way of value. These sales are blind and have very little value, especially if the company is a nonreporting company and is not subject to federal reporting requirements.

In either event, the restriction relates to sales by officers and directors, and any private sale of these stocks based on either time or profitability would likely be subject to little in the way of warranties concerning the value of stock then transferred. As such, sale would not be subject to a lawsuit for fraud and misrepresentation, if the officer or director was engaged in the same. And of course, it turns out that is what they were engaged in doing. One wonders why one would buy such a stock other than for pure speculation. This is especially true in light of the facts as revealed by the investigation of TelexGlobal for criminal activity. If Mr. Molitor or Mr. Yount had tried to sell restricted TelexGlobal shares in a market suspicious of its integrity, he would have had to give it away.

In addition, Dr. Singley relies on two types of studies unrelated to the market for TelexGlobal's stock. The first studies are sales of restricted stock in relationship to future known sales of stock in initial public offerings of that same stock. There was no indication in the record that TelexGlobal was contemplating an IPO for its stock. Purchases of restricted stock in a run-up to an IPO have other protections that impact the value someone might pay for such stock. These stocks have to go through public reporting requirements, and the issuers are subject to federal securities law if they make misrepresentations.

In contrast, TelexGlobal was selling restricted shares that represented the value of its recently purchased Huba Hub Link, a private telemarketing company based out of Canada. Any purchaser of this stock would have no public record of what it was purchasing, nor could it expect to receive one in the future.

As a result of the above, the specific marketability of TGLC cannot be compared to statistics drawn from data from sales of restricted stock from public reporting companies or from companies about to raise money through an IPO.

An averaging of unreliable studies does not produce a basis to average the methods.

Value of Stocks Based on MMG Shareholder Report

In my opinion, basing the reasonableness of Dr. Singley's expert opinion on Mr. Molitor's own statements in his investor newsletter misunderstands the nature of those statements. Most sophisticated investors understand that they are not to place reliance on any future-oriented statements made in these reports. While some of the statements in the report are written as statements of present value, they of course inherently also contain expectations of the happening of future events: 1) that the company is not engaged in illegal activity, or 2) that the restrictions for the stock will be lifted in due course. The happening of these events, while implicit in the statements concerning the present value of these stocks, are not meant to be relied on by the investors of the fund. They know that. And even if they do not, the disclaimer at the bottom of the fund newsletter makes it undeniable. I quote from the letter, below:

> Statements made in this fund report, other than those concerning historical information, should be considered forward looking and subject to various risks and uncertainties. Such forward-looking statements are made based on management's belief, as well as assumptions made by and information currently available to, management pursuant to the "safe harbor" provisions of certain federal and state laws and regulations. Actual results may differ materially from the results anticipated in these forward-looking statements as a result of a variety of factors. Additional information concerning these factors may be found on some of the companies' website, as well

as, in the case of certain companies, their periodic public filings with the Securities and Exchange Commission. The Fund undertakes no obligation to update the statements contained in this fund report after the date hereof.

The value of the Fund's investments will vary from day to day in response to many factors. Values fluctuate in response to the activities of individual companies, and general market and economic conditions. You may have a gain or loss when you sell your shares. Investments in foreign companies, especially those in emerging markets, involve risks in addition to those of U.S. investments, including increased political and economic risk, as well as exposure to currency fluctuations. Since the fund is aggressive in its search for capital appreciation, share price may vary significantly with changing market and industry conditions. Share price may also be more volatile than a fund that diversifies across may industry sections and companies. Past performance is no guarantee of future results.

Curriculum Vitae

Dr. Jamie R. Connors, PhD, CFF, CPA, CFE
President, Valuation Vault, LLC
127 Newberry St., Central, Nita 01514
(555) 225-3304

Current Position

Co-founder and President of Valuation Vault, LLC

Professional History

Valuation Vault, LLC President

Securities & Exchange Commission, Deputy Chief Accountant, YR-18 – YR-14

Deloitte, LLP, Senior Director Business Valuation Team, YR-20 – YR-18

Deloitte, LLP, Senior Associate Business Valuation Team, YR-24 – YR-20

University of Chicago, Assistant Professor in Economics, YR-29 – YR-24

General Electric, Corporate Financial Planning and Analysis, YR-30 – YR-29

Practice Areas

Litigation Consulting and Expert Testimony – Retained in over 400 matters on behalf of defendants; damage calculations in business torts and antitrust cases; economic analysis in white-collar fraud and fraud on the market matters

Valuation Services – Appraise closely held corporations, partnerships, and various business entities; intellectual property and goodwill analysis

Corporate Planning and Analysis – Certify integrity of financial statements; analyze short-term capitalization options for distressed clients and financing options for expanding ones

Data Collection – Collect and analyze data on executive compensation, industry pricing and production levels, and best practices

Recent Expert Testimony

Mitchell v. Cantone	Trial	YR-1	Nita
Tech4Now v. Young Technologies	Trial	YR-1	Nita
Greenbaum v. New York Jets	Trial	YR-2	New York
City of Dallas v. CRE Finance Council	Deposition	YR-2	Texas
Microsoft v. Seattle University	Deposition and Trial	YR-2	Washington
Stoller, et al. v. Young Technologies	Arbitration	YR-2	Nita
Benfield v. Boston Securities Traders Organization	Deposition and Trial	YR-3	Nita
The Andover Companies v. Gutierrez	Arbitration	YR-3	Nita

Professional Memberships, Affiliations, and Accomplishments

- Certified Public Accountant (CPA)
- Certified Financial Advisor (CFA)
- Certified Fraud Examiner (CFE)
- American Institute of Certified Public Accountants
- Nita Association of Certified Public Accountants
- Association of Certified Fraud Examiners
- National Association of Certified Valuators and Analysts
- Nita Biotechnology Council
- Central Securities Traders Organization
- AICPA, Accredited in Business Valuation, ABV
- AICPA, Certified in Financial Forensics, CFF
- University of Chicago, Visiting Lecturer on the macro-economic ramifications of financial fraud, YR-7
- Greater Central Chamber of Commerce Academy of Distinguished Centralians, Inductee
- Advisor to the Office of the Comptroller, Central University
- Authored editorials in the *New York Times*, *Boston Globe*, and other media outlets
- Authored *A Statistical Analysis of Corporate Valuation*, self-published in YR-5
- Co-author of *My Time at the Securities and Exchange Commission: Case Studies of a Financial Regulator* (forthcoming)
- Listed in *Central* magazine's "100 People Who Run this Town" in YR-1

Community Service

Chairman, Salvation Army Advisory Board

Trustee, Franklin Park Zoo

Board of Trustees, Catholic Charities

Education

Doctor of Philosophy in Economics, Nita State University

Master of Science in Mathematics, Bachelor of Science in Business Administration, Furman University, YR-36; Concentration in Accounting and Statistical Analysis

EXHIBITS

Exhibit 1

Original Severance Agreement

Severance Agreement

- In lieu of $7,212 owed to Stephen F. Yount (SFY) by Molitor Management Group, Inc. (MMG), SFY will purchase from MMG and Harold B. Molitor for said amount the following interests:
- Insured Communications, Inc. – 12.5% of MMG's interest after deducting Molitor Technology's Fund 20% sharing agreement
- Roucher Central/Roucher Motors – 12.5% of MMG's interest after deducting Molitor Technology's Fund 20% sharing agreement
- Enginuity Software, Inc. – 187 shares currently held by MMG
- Nevada Software Technology Applications, Inc. – 12,500 shares of Harold A. Molitor's interest
- TelPower Corporation – 12.4% of MMG's interest
- RWS – 10% of MMG's interest
- TelexGlobal Corp. – 192,030 shares currently held by MMG
- The Technology Group, Inc. – 1,613 warrants currently held by MMG

The above represents final obligations between Stephen F. Yount, Molitor Management Group, Inc. and Harold A. Molitor. Harold Molitor will cause those interests above currently in his or MMG's possession to be transferred to SFY by May 31, YR-5, with the remainder to be transferred concurrent with, or within ten days of receipt by HAM or MMG.

Agreed 4/30/YR-5

/s/
Fred D. Yount

Molitor Management Group, Inc.

/s/
Harold A. Molitor, Chairman

Harold A. Molitor, As Individual

Exhibit 2

Screenshot of Harold Molitor's Facebook Page, October 2, YR-4

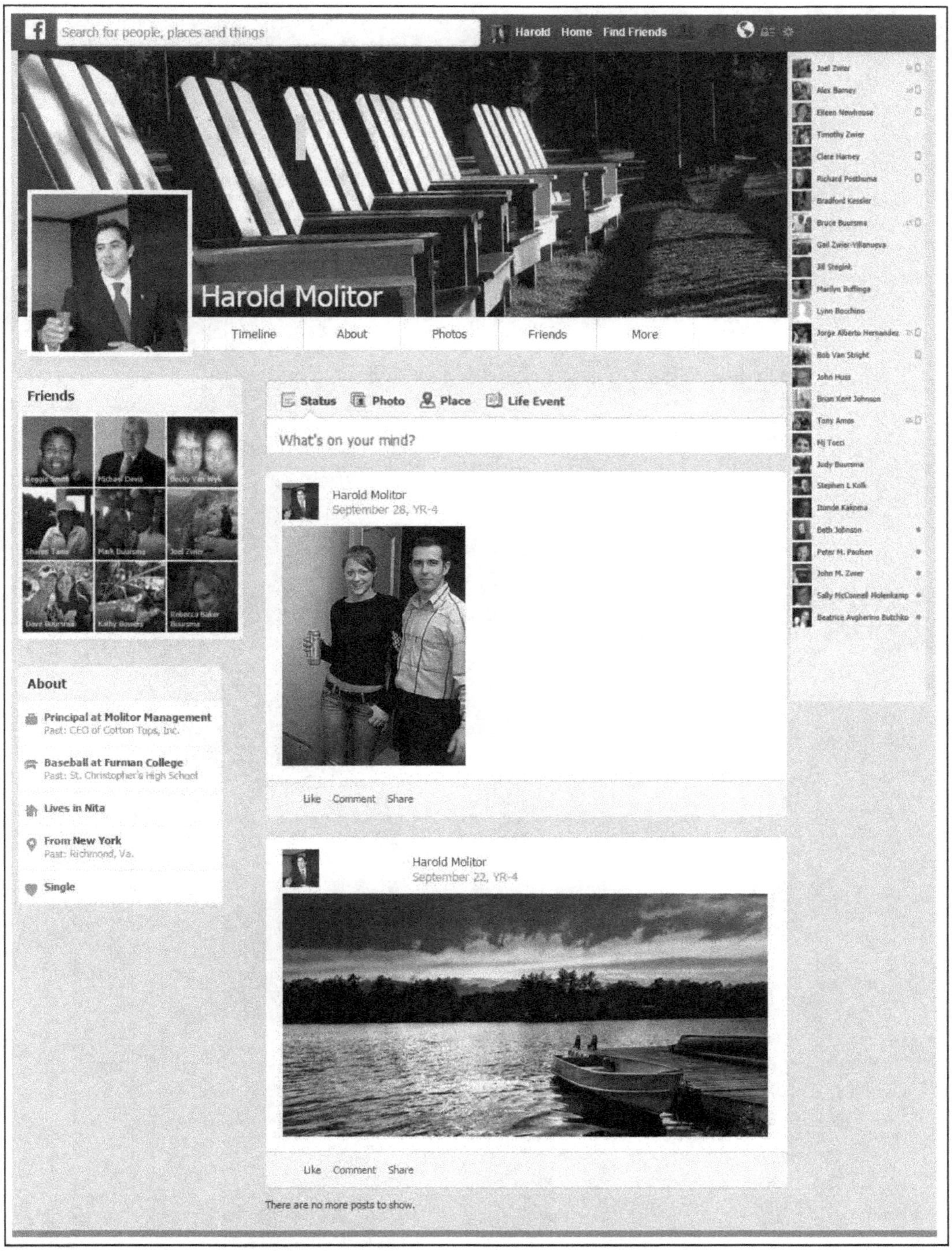

See http://bit.ly/1Dv2ecl.

Exhibit 3

Email from Harold Molitor to Susan Durham, September 30, YR-4

RE: Last Night

Harold Molitor

Sent: September 30, YR-4

To: Susan Durham

Message

Dear Susan,

So you saw the picture I posted of Facebook of you and Stephen. I'll take it down. Wasn't sure you would remember. Wow, what a night last night. You know, we went through three bottles of wine! We have had some pretty wild times out at the lake house, haven't we? I have to admit you sure looked great in those jeans. And I have been kicking myself for not finding a way to take you up on your offer. It is really flattering for an old guy like me to be propositioned by a beautiful young woman like you. If I were a younger man… Look, I know that you and Stephen are going through a rough patch. I promise we are going to come out of this economic downturn better than ever. And haven't I always taken care of you two?

- Hal

Exhibit 4

Unsigned Amended Severance Agreement, with List of Stock

AMENDMENT TO SEVERANCE AGREEMENT

Stephen F. Yount (SFY), Molitor Management Group, Inc. (MMG), and Harold A. Molitor, parties to SFY's Severance Agreement dated April 30, YR-5, for good and valuable consideration, (including but not limited to their original promises and the mutual promises set forth herein), the receipt and sufficiency of which is hereby acknowledged, agree as follows:

The original May 31, YR-5, date, by which Harold Molitor was obligated to cause certain enumerated interests to be transferred to SFY is extended to January 31, YR-3. Harold Molitor will cause those enumerated interests to be transferred to SFY on or before January 31, YR-3. To the extent Harold Molitor or MMG do not yet have possession or control of those interests as of the date for transfer, Harold Molitor will cause those interests or any remaining portion thereof, to be transferred to SFY within ten days of receipt by him or by MMG. All other terms of the Severance Agreement shall remain unchanged.

____

Stephen F. Yount

____

Molitor Management Group, Inc., by its Chairman
Harold A. Molitor, and Harold A. Molitor, individually

List of Stock

- Insured Communications, Inc. – 12.5% of MMG's interest after deducting Molitor Technology's Fund 20% sharing agreement.
- Roucher Central/Roucher Motors – 12.5% of MMG's interest after deducting Molitor Technology's Fund 20% sharing agreement.
- Engineous Software, Inc. – 187 shares currently held by MMG
- Nevada Software Technology Applications, Inc. – 12,500 shares of Harold A. Molitor's interest (now known as Standard TECH)
- TelPower Corporation – 12.4% of MMG's interest
- TMS – 10% of MMG's interest
- TelexGlobalCorp – 192,030 shares currently held by MMG
- The Technology Group, Inc. – 1,613 warrants currently held by MMG

Exhibit 5

Yount's Camera Phone Photo of Signed Agreement, Undated

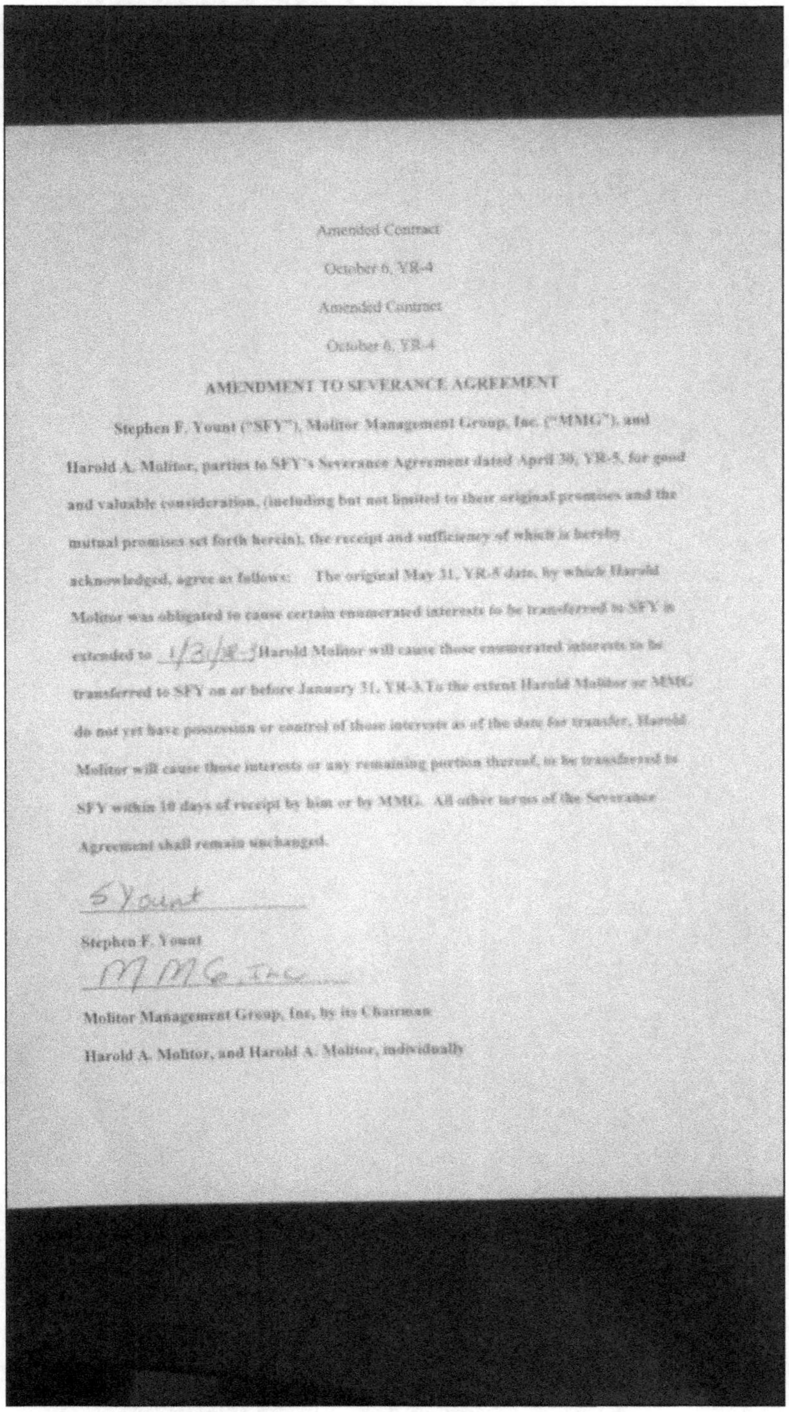

Amended Contract

October 6, YR-4

Amended Contract

October 6, YR-4

AMENDMENT TO SEVERANCE AGREEMENT

Stephen F. Yount ("SFY"), Molitor Management Group, Inc. ("MMG"), and Harold A. Molitor, parties to SFY's Severance Agreement dated April 30, YR-5, for good and valuable consideration, (including but not limited to their original promises and the mutual promises set forth herein), the receipt and sufficiency of which is hereby acknowledged, agree as follows: The original May 31, YR-5 date, by which Harold Molitor was obligated to cause certain enumerated interests to be transferred to SFY is extended to 1/31/YR-3 **Harold Molitor will cause those enumerated interests to be transferred to SFY on or before January 31, YR-3.To the extent Harold Molitor or MMG do not yet have possession or control of those interests as of the date for transfer, Harold Molitor will cause those interests or any remaining portion thereof, to be transferred to SFY within 10 days of receipt by him or by MMG. All other terms of the Severance Agreement shall remain unchanged.**

S Yount

Stephen F. Yount

MMG, Inc.

Molitor Management Group, Inc, by its Chairman

Harold A. Molitor, and Harold A. Molitor, individually

Exhibit 6

Text Message from Stephen Yount to Susan Durham, October 6, YR-4

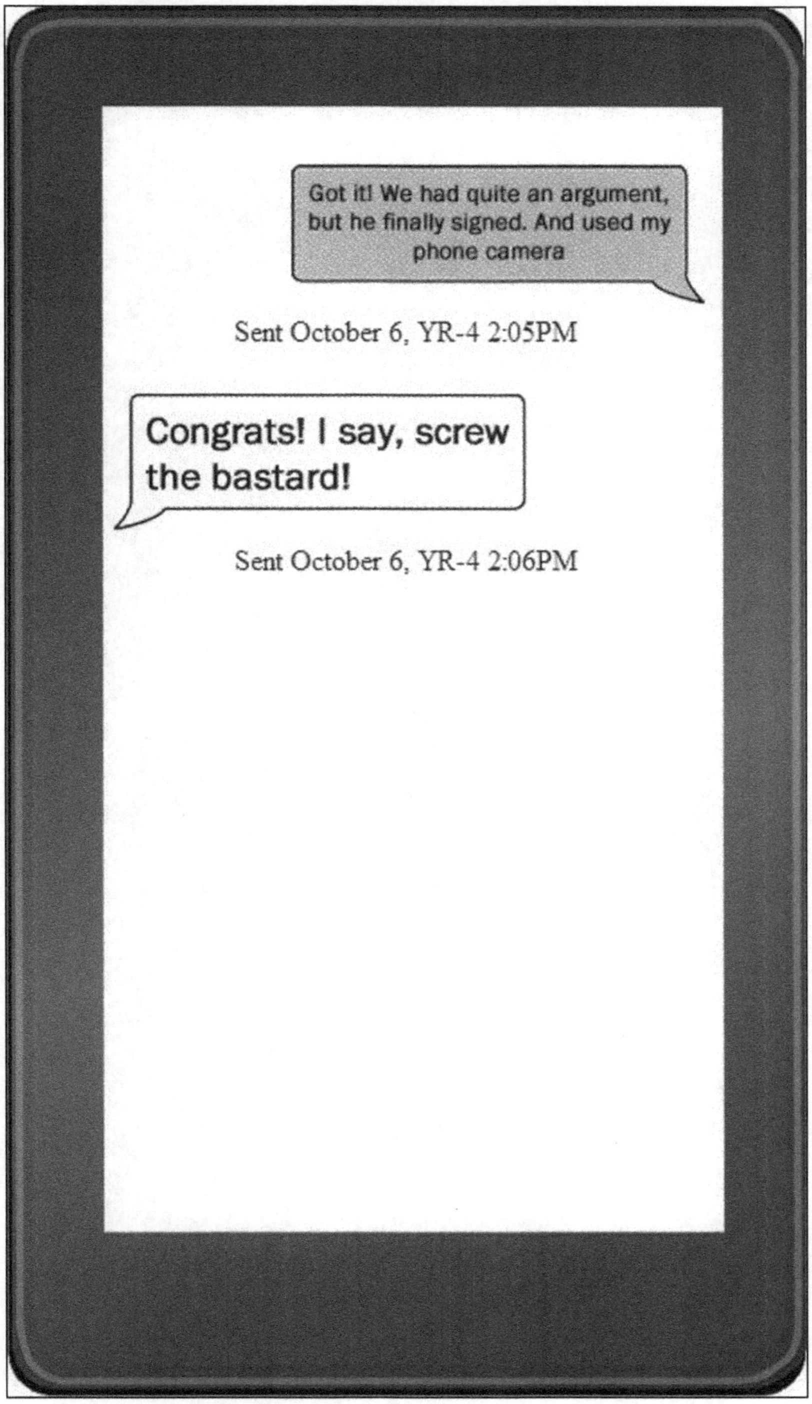

See http://bit.ly/1kXTlDC.

Exhibit 7

Susan Durham's Camera Phone Photo of Signed Amendment to Severance Agreement, October 7, YR-4

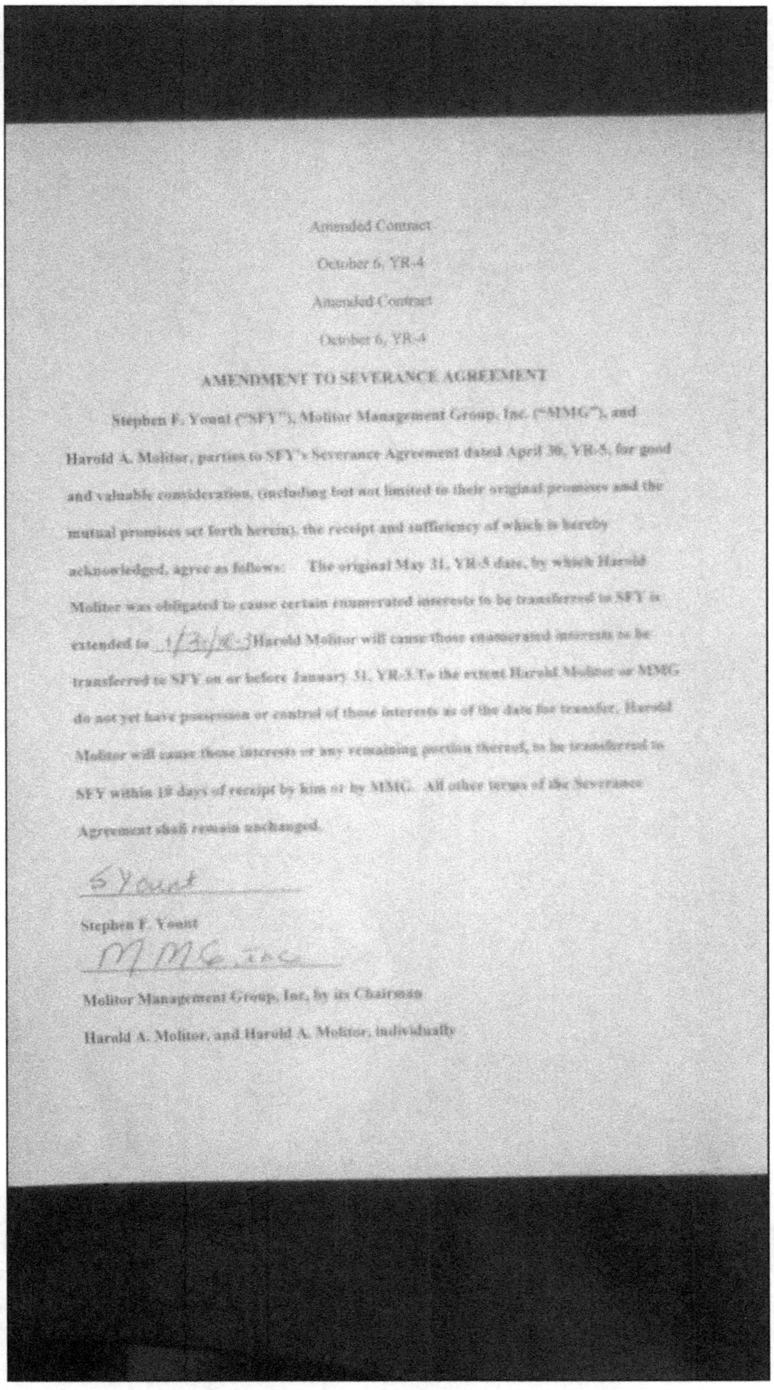

Amended Contract

October 6, YR-4

Amended Contract

October 6, YR-4

AMENDMENT TO SEVERANCE AGREEMENT

Stephen F. Yount ("SFY"), Molitor Management Group, Inc. ("MMG"), and Harold A. Molitor, parties to SFY's Severance Agreement dated April 30, YR-5, for good and valuable consideration, (including but not limited to their original promises and the mutual promises set forth herein), the receipt and sufficiency of which is hereby acknowledged, agree as follows: The original May 31, YR-5 date, by which Harold Molitor was obligated to cause certain enumerated interests to be transferred to SFY is extended to 1/31/YR-3 Harold Molitor will cause those enumerated interests to be transferred to SFY on or before January 31, YR-3.To the extent Harold Molitor or MMG do not yet have possession or control of those interests as of the date for transfer, Harold Molitor will cause those interests or any remaining portion thereof, to be transferred to SFY within 10 days of receipt by him or by MMG. All other terms of the Severance Agreement shall remain unchanged.

S Yount

Stephen F. Yount

MMG, Inc.

Molitor Management Group, Inc, by its Chairman

Harold A. Molitor, and Harold A. Molitor, individually

Exhibit 8

Restricted—Stock Certificate, TelexGlobal

The shares represented by this certificate have not been registered under the Securities Act of 1933, as amended, or any applicable state securities laws and may not be transferred, sold, or assigned unless so registered or unless an exemption from such registration is available.

Certificate Number 000865 192,030 Shares

INCORPORATED UNDER THE LAWS OF DELAWARE

TELEXGLOBAL

This certifies that Harold Molitor owns 192,030 shares of no par value common stock of Standard Mems, transferable only on the books of the corporation by the holder of this certificate in person, or by authorized agent, upon surrender of this certificate, properly endorsed.

Restricted

In witness of the above, the corporation has caused this certificate to be signed by its authorized officers on May 01, YR-5.

________________________ ________________________

Paul J. Zwier, President William Hunt, Secretary

Transfer Section

For value received, I, Harold Molitor, transfer to ____________________ the shares represented by this certificate, and instruct the corporate Secretary to record this transfer on the books of the corporation. Transfer restrictions, if any, are shown above.

Dated this ____ day of __________, YR-____.

____

Harold Molitor

Exhibit 9

Stock Certificate—Standard TECH

Certificate Number 000123 12,500 Shares

INCORPORATED UNDER THE LAWS OF DELAWARE

NEVADA SOFTWARE TECHNOLOGY APPLICATIONS (STANDARD TECH)

This certifies that Harold Molitor owns 192,030 shares of no par value common stock of Standard Mems, transferable only on the books of the corporation by the holder of this certificate in person, or by authorized agent, upon surrender of this certificate, properly endorsed.

In witness of the above, the corporation has caused this certificate to be signed by its authorized officers on JUNE 15, YR-5.

________________________ ________________________

Robert Trammel, President Alan Whitaker, Secretary

Transfer Section

For value received, I, Harold Molitor, transfer to ____________________ the shares represented by this certificate, and instruct the corporate Secretary to record this transfer on the books of the corporation. Transfer restrictions, if any, are shown above.

Dated this ____ day of ____________, YR-____.

____

Harold Molitor

Exhibit 10

Molitor Management Fund Balance Sheet, December YR-4

Molitor Technology Fund I Valuation
End of Year Two of a Five-Year Life
December 31, YR-4

Company	12/31/YR-4 Value	Shares	Per Share Cost	12/31/YR-3 Value	Gain (Loss)	Percent Change
Standard TECH	$ 500,000	500,000	$12.50	$ 6,250,000	$5,750,000	1150%
HubaHubLink	550,000	2,091,588	1-11/16	3,529,555	2,979,555	542%
Roucher	200,000	500,000	2.00	1,000,000	800,000	400%
IXATA Group (IXTA)	115,000	59,300	0.12	7,116	(107,884)	–94%
Power Oasis	50,000	1	1.00	1	(49,999)	–100%
Third Millenium Systems	150,000	1	1.00	1	(149,999)	–100%
	$ 1,565,000			**$10,786,673**	**$ 9,221,673**	**589%**

Cash	**5,000**
Total Assets	**10,791,673**
Expenses payable—primarily management fees	**(353,000)**
Net Asset Value	**$10,438,673**
Total Shares	**1,600,000**
Net Asset Value of $1.00 Shares	**$6.52**
Net Asset Value of $50,000 Unit (32 total units)	**$326,209**
Total Gain—Two Years	**552%**

Exhibit 11

Molitor Management Fund Newsletter

MOLITOR TECHNOLOGY MANAGEMENT CORP.
24 Yardley Executive Park
Yardley, Nita

Molitor Technology Fund, L.P.
Fund Report
For the Fourth Quarter and
Year Ended December 31, YR-4

January 17, YR-3

Dear Molitor Technology Fund, L.P. Investor:

Executive Summary

The Molitor Technology Fund, L.P. ended the fourth quarter with a Net Asset Value of $10,439,000. Each $50,000 unit had a value of $326,000 as of December 31, YR-4.

General

The year has been a market rollercoaster ride, to say the least! While the unit value is down from its peak, we are thrilled to report a valuation that ends up showing a gain of over 550 percent for the two years since inception.

Investment Highlights

Standard TECH

The company is executing on its business plan, which translates directly into its increased value. They are currently completing a private placement led by Piper Jaffray at $12.50 per share.

We believe that the prospect of an IPO are still bright, but may be impacted by future capital market conditions. The company believes a May/June YR-4 time frame for the IPO is possible; however, our feeling is that September/October YR-4 is more likely.

In September YR-4, Standard TECH and Phillips Semiconductors, a division of Royal Phillips electronics, announced a joint venture to build a $160 million manufacturing facility in Germany for Tech products. This investment is important for the future growth and success of the company as it moves to execute its global strategy. The company expects the first silicon will be produced in the second half of YR-3. The CMOS and TECH wafers produced in the facility are to supply the rapidly growing wireless/cellular and pager telecommunications and other markets. In addition, the facility will serve as a leading-edge R&D base.

In November, Standard TECH announced the acquisition of Xicor, Inc.'s (NASDAQ/NMS: XICO) Milpitas, California, silicon foundry. With this acquisition, Standard TECH, Inc., now offers the most complete TECH production capability in the world.

In December, Standard TECH and the Center for Automation Technologies (CAT) at Rensselaer Polytechnic Institute joined forces to create a joint micropackaging research and development program. This strategic alliance between the company, the largest independent high-volume manufacturer of micropackaging, CAT, the leading North American university-based, industry-driven automation R&D center, will focus on the development and prototyping of state of the art micromanufacturing technologies giving customers leading-edge packaging solutions.

TelexGlobal Corporation

Recently, TelexGlobal closed at $2.91 per share (on January 16), as compared to the $1-11/16 value in December 31, YR-4 fund report; let's hope the trend continues!

The company has made significant progress in two business areas: wireless encryption and the Internet customer care service center. The company's wireless encryption business recently completed the Field Programmable Gate Array (FPGA) board aimed at securing all voice and data transmissions through wireless devices such as cellular phones. WorldWideAssist, the company's Internet customer care business, recently completed a technology implementation, offering customer resource management (CRM) to potential clients.

In January YR-3, the company relocated to its new corporate office at One Technology Drive, Andover, Nita from Burlington, Nita.

Roucher Central

Hans Roucher, the founder, visited us in December and advised that the company is on target with its business plan. The Fund owns one hundred percent of Roucher Central, which in turn owns fourteen percent of Roucher Germany, the "operating company." Hanover Bank (Germany) and Roucher Germany recently completed an equity financing that valued Roucher Germany at $15 million. Using that valuation as a base and our fourteen percent position in Roucher Germany (through our Blocker Central ownership), our investment value is approximately $2.1 million. However, due to the company being an early state technology entity and the challenges in achieving market acceptance and penetration in global markets with established competitors, we have decided to reduce the carrying value of the company by approximately fifty percent, thereby recording it at a $1 million value in December 31, YR-4, Fund valuation.

The development of Roucher's second product, the miniaturized frequency converter, is well on its way and has received high levels of interest. We remain confident of the significant opportunity that the company can leverage during YR-3 and beyond as it executes on its plans to produce and deliver product and gain increased market acceptance and penetration for its revolutionizing technology.

Molitor Technology Fund II, LP

Currently, there are exciting developments in Molitor Technology Fund II, which is further explained in Fund II's first annual report, which is enclosed. The investment committee of Fund II has agreed to a forty-five-day investment period extension, during which time, original investment class shares are still available at $1.00 per share.

If you would like to invest in Fund II, please contact Beverly O'Connor in our office for a copy of the appropriate documents.

Very truly yours,

Harold A. Molitor
Portfolio Manager & President

Michael Dewar
Director

SFY:HAM:bao

Safe Harbor for Forward Looking Statements and Risk Factors

Statements made in this fund report, other than those concerning historical information, should be considered forward looking and subject to various risks and uncertainties. Such forward-looking statements are made based on management's belief, as well as assumptions made by and information currently available to, management pursuant to the "safe harbor" provisions of certain federal and state laws and regulations. Actual results may differ materially from the results anticipated in these forward-looking statements as a result of a variety of factors. Additional information concerning these factors may be found on some of the companies' website as well as, in the case of certain companies, their periodic public filings with the Securities and Exchange Commission. The Fund undertakes no obligation to update the statements contained in this fund report after the date hereof.

The value of the Fund's investments will vary from day to day in response to many factors. Values fluctuate in response to the activities of individual companies and general market and economic conditions. You may have a gain or loss when you sell your shares. Investments in foreign companies, especially those in emerging markets, involve risks in addition to those of U.S. investments, including increased political and economic risk as well as exposure to currency fluctuations. Since the fund is aggressive in its search for capital appreciation, share price may vary significantly with changing market and industry conditions. Share price may also be more volatile than a fund that diversifies across may industry sections and companies. Past performance is no guarantee of future results.

Exhibit 12

SEC Rule 144 (Learned Treatise)

Rule 144: Selling Restricted and Control Securities

When you acquire restricted securities or hold control securities, you must find an exemption from the SEC's registration requirements to sell them in a public marketplace. Rule 144 allows public resale of restricted and control securities if a number of conditions are met. This overview tells you what you need to know about selling your restricted or control securities. It also describes how to have a restrictive legend removed.

What Are Restricted and Control Securities?

Restricted securities are securities acquired in unregistered, private sales from the issuing company or from an affiliate of the issuer. Investors typically receive restricted securities through private placement offerings, Regulation D offerings, employee stock benefit plans, as compensation for professional services, or in exchange for providing "seed money" or start-up capital to the company. Rule 144(a)(3) identifies what sales produce restricted securities.

Control securities are those held by an affiliate of the issuing company. An affiliate is a person, such as an executive officer, a director or large shareholder, in a relationship of control with the issuer. Control means the power to direct the management and policies of the company in question, whether through the ownership of voting securities, by contract, or otherwise. If you buy securities from a controlling person or "affiliate," you take restricted securities, even if they were not restricted in the affiliate's hands.

If you acquire restrictive securities, you almost always will receive a certificate stamped with a "restrictive" legend. The legend indicates that the securities may not be resold in the marketplace unless they are registered with the SEC or are exempt from the registration requirements. Certificates for control securities usually are not stamped with a legend.

What Are the Conditions of Rule 144?

If you want to sell your restricted or control securities to the public, you can meet the applicable conditions set forth in Rule 144. The rule is not the exclusive means for selling restricted or control securities, but provides a "safe harbor" exemption to sellers. The rule's five conditions are summarized below:

Additional securities purchased from the issuer do not affect the holding period of previously purchased securities of the same class. If you purchased restricted securities from another non-affiliate, you can tack on that non-affiliate's holding period to your holding period. For gifts made by an affiliate, the holding period begins when the affiliate acquired the securities and not on the date of the gift. In the case of a stock option, including employee stock options, the holding period begins on the date the option is exercised and not the date it is granted.

1. **Holding Period**. Before you may sell any restricted securities in the marketplace, you must hold them for a certain period of time. If the company that issued the securities is a "reporting company" in that it is subject to the reporting requirements of the Securities Exchange Act of 1934, then you must hold the securities for at least six months. If the issuer of the securities is not subject to the reporting requirements, then you must hold the securities for at least one year. The relevant holding period begins when the securities

were bought and fully paid for. The holding period only applies to restricted securities. Because securities acquired in the public market are not restricted, there is no holding period for an affiliate who purchases securities of the issuer in the marketplace. But the resale of an affiliate's shares as control securities is subject to the other conditions of the rule.

2. **Current Public Information**. There must be adequate current information about the issuing company publicly available before the sale can be made. For reporting companies, this generally means that the companies have complied with the periodic reporting requirements of the Securities Exchange Act of 1934. For non-reporting companies, this means that certain company information, including information regarding the nature of its business, the identity of its officers and directors, and its financial statements, is publicly available.
3. **Trading Volume Formula**. If you are an affiliate, the number of equity securities you may sell during any three-month period cannot exceed the greater of 1% of the outstanding shares of the same class being sold, or if the class is listed on a stock exchange, the greater of 1% or the average reported weekly trading volume during the four weeks preceding the filing of a notice of sale on Form 144. Over-the-counter stocks, including those quoted on the OTC Bulletin Board and the Pink Sheets, can only be sold using the 1% measurement.
4. **Ordinary Brokerage Transactions**. If you are an affiliate, the sales must be handled in all respects as routine trading transactions, and brokers may not receive more than a normal commission. Neither the seller nor the broker can solicit orders to buy the securities.
5. **Filing a Notice of Proposed Sale With the SEC**. If you are an affiliate, you must file a notice with the SEC on Form 144 if the sale involves more than 5,000 shares or the aggregate dollar amount is greater than $50,000 in any three-month period.

If I Am Not an Affiliate of the Issuer, What Conditions of Rule 144 Must I Comply With?

If you are not (and have not been for at least three months) an affiliate of the company issuing the securities and have held the restricted securities for at least one year, you can sell the securities without regard to the conditions in Rule 144 discussed above. If the issuer of the securities is subject to the Exchange Act reporting requirements and you have held the securities for at least six months but less than one year, you may sell the securities as long as you satisfy the current public information condition.

Can the Securities Be Sold Publicly If the Conditions of Rule 144 Have Been Met?

Even if you have met the conditions of Rule 144, you can't sell your restricted securities to the public until you've gotten the legend removed from the certificate. Only a transfer agent can remove a restrictive legend. But the transfer agent won't remove the legend unless you've obtained the consent of the issuer—usually in the form of an opinion letter from the issuer's counsel—that the restrictive legend can be removed. Unless this happens, the transfer agent doesn't have the authority to remove the legend and permit execution of the trade in the marketplace.

To begin the legend removal process, an investor should contact the company that issued the securities, or the transfer agent for the securities, to ask about the procedures for removing a legend. Removing the legend can be a complicated process requiring you to work with an attorney who specializes in securities law.

What If a Dispute Arises Over Whether I Can Remove the Legend?

If a dispute arises about whether a restrictive legend can be removed, the SEC will not intervene. Removal of a legend is a matter solely in the discretion of the issuer of the securities. State law, not federal law, covers disputes about the removal of legends. Thus, the SEC will not take action in any decision or dispute about removing a restrictive legend.

> The Office of Investor Education and Advocacy has provided this information as a service to investors. It is neither a legal interpretation nor a statement of SEC policy. If you have questions concerning the meaning or application of a particular law or rule, please consult with an attorney who specializes in securities law.

Modified: Jan. 16, 2013

Jury Instructions and Verdict Form

JURY INSTRUCTIONS

PRELIMINARY INSTRUCTIONS

Nita Instruction 1:01 — Introduction

You have been selected as jurors and have taken an oath to well and truly try this cause. This trial will last one day. During the progress of the trial, there will be periods of time when the Court recesses. During those periods of time, you must not talk about this case among yourselves or with anyone else.

During the trial, do not talk to any of the parties, their lawyers, or any of the witnesses. If any attempt is made by anyone to talk to you concerning the matters here under consideration, you should immediately report that fact to the Court. You should keep an open mind. You should not form or express an opinion during the trial and should reach no conclusion in this case until you have heard all of the evidence, the arguments of counsel, and the final instructions as to the law that will be given to you by the Court.

Nita Instruction 1:02 — Conduct of the Trial

First, the attorneys will have an opportunity to make opening statements. These statements are not evidence and should be considered only as a preview of what the attorneys expect the evidence will be. Following the opening statements, witnesses will be called to testify. They will be placed under oath and questioned by the attorneys. Documents and other tangible exhibits may also be received as evidence. If an exhibit is given to you to examine, you should examine it carefully, individually, and without any comment.

It is counsel's right and duty to object when testimony or other evidence is being offered that he or she believes is not admissible. When the court sustains an objection to a question, the jurors must disregard the question and the answer, if one has been given, and draw no inference from the question or answer or speculate as to what the witness would have said if permitted to answer. Jurors must also disregard evidence stricken from the record. When the Court sustains an objection to any evidence, the jurors must disregard that evidence. When the court overrules an objection to any evidence, the jurors must not give that evidence any more weight than if the objection had not been made.

When the evidence is completed, the attorneys will make final statements. These final statements are not evidence, but are given to help you evaluate the evidence. The attorneys are also permitted to argue in an attempt to persuade you to a particular verdict. You may accept or reject those arguments as you see fit. Finally, just before you retire to consider your verdict, the Court will give you further instructions on the law that applies to this case.

Final Instructions

Nita Instruction 2:01 — Introduction

Members of the jury, the evidence and arguments in this case have been completed, and I will now instruct you as to the law. The law applicable to this case is stated in these instructions, and it is your duty to follow all of these instructions. You must not single out certain ones and disregard others. It is your duty to determine the facts and to determine them only from the evidence in this case. You are to apply the law to the facts and in this way decide the case. You must not be governed or influenced by sympathy or prejudice for or against any party in this case. Your verdict must be based on evidence and not on speculation, guess, or conjecture. The evidence that you should consider consists only of the testimony of the witnesses testimonies and the exhibits the court has received. Any evidence that was received for a limited purpose should not be considered by you for any other purpose. You should consider all the evidence in the light of your own observations and experiences in life.

Nita Instruction 2:02 — Opening Statements and Closing Arguments

Opening statements are made by the attorneys to acquaint you with the facts they expect to prove. Closing arguments are made by the attorneys to discuss the facts and circumstances in the case and should be confined to the evidence and to reasonable inferences to be drawn therefrom. Neither opening statements nor closing arguments are evidence, and any statement or argument made by the attorneys that is not based on the evidence should be disregarded.

Nita Instruction 2:03 — Credibility of the Witnesses

You are the sole judges of the credibility of the witnesses and of the weight to be given to the testimony of each witness. When determining what credit is to be given any witness, you may take into account his ability and opportunity to observe; his manner and appearance while testifying; any interest, bias, or prejudice he may have; the reasonableness of his testimony considered in the light of all the evidence; and any other factors that bear on the believability and weight of the witness's testimony.

Nita Instruction 2:04 — Direct and Circumstantial Evidence

The law recognizes two kinds of evidence: direct and circumstantial. Direct evidence proves a fact directly; that is, the evidence by itself, if true, establishes the fact. Circumstantial evidence is the proof of facts or circumstances that give rise to a reasonable inference of other facts; that is, circumstantial evidence proves a fact indirectly in that it follows from other facts or circumstances according to common experience and observations in life. An eyewitness is a common example of direct evidence, while human footprints are circumstantial evidence that a person was present.

The law makes no distinction between direct and circumstantial evidence regarding the degree or amount of proof required, and you should consider and evaluate each to arrive at your verdict.

Nita Instruction 2:05 — Burden of Proof

When I say that a party has the burden of proof on any issue, or use the expression "if you find" or "if you decide" or "by a preponderance of evidence," I mean that you must be persuaded from a consideration of all the evidence in the case that the issue in question is more probably true than not true. Any findings of fact you make must be based on probabilities, not possibilities. It may not be based on surmise, speculation, or conjecture.

Proposed Jury Instructions

Specific to the Case

1. Introduction

The court will now instruct you on the claims and defenses of each party and the law governing the case. You must arrive at your verdict by applying the law, as I now instruct you, to the facts as you find them to be.

2. Background—Basic Contentions of the Parties

The parties to this case are Stephen F. Yount, the plaintiff, and Harold Molitor, and the Molitor Management Group, Inc., (MMG), the defendants. Stephen F. Yount has sued the defendants seeking to recover damages based on a claim that the defendants failed to transfer stock pursuant to a severance agreement the parties had entered into, which was then subject to a claimed extension of that agreement from May 31, YR-5, to January 31, YR-3. Both sides agree that the listed stocks, attached to the document initially entitled "Severance Agreement," were never transferred to the plaintiff. The defendants deny that there was ever a contract to transfer the stock because the severance agreement was intended as a gift, and as a gift, the transfer lacked any legal consideration required to make it a contract. In addition, the defendant claims that the extension was never agreed to between the parties. The defendant also argues that in the alternative, even if the agreement was a contract, and even if it had been extended, all of the shares listed had no market value; further, the defendant argues that even if one of the stock may have had value, it was restricted stock, and as such could not have had the restrictions removed and sold within the time specified by the agreement for transfer.

3. Damages—General

If the plaintiff prevails, his damages will be predicated on the value of the listed stock attached to the severance agreement. The plaintiff must prove the value of each stock during the time of the severance agreement.

4. Existence of a Contract

You first must decide whether the plaintiff has proven that there was a contract for the exchange of stock. For there to have been a contract, the plaintiff must have given consideration for the defendant's promise exchange stock. Consideration is defined as follows:

> Something of value given by both parties to a contract that induces them to enter into the agreement to exchange mutual performances.

Consideration is an essential element for the formation of a contract. It may consist of a promise to perform a desired act or a promise to refrain from doing an act that one is legally entitled to do. In a bilateral contract—an agreement by which both parties exchange mutual promises—each promise is regarded as sufficient consideration for the other. In a unilateral contract, an agreement by which one party makes a promise in exchange for the other's performance, the performance is consideration for the promise, while the promise is consideration for the performance. In a unilateral contract, the promise is due once the performance has been complete.

Consideration must have a value that can be objectively determined. A promise, for example, to make a gift or a promise of love or affection is not enforceable because of the subjective nature of the promise.

An exchange of mutual promises provides the basis for a contract. One party is said to make an offer and the other promises by accepting the offer. Whether there was mutual assent must be determined from the conduct of parties. No writing is required. Whether that conduct constituted an offer and acceptance—and, if it did, what its meaning was—depends on what reasonable persons in the positions of the parties would have thought they meant. In determining what reasonable persons would have thought the conduct meant, you should consider the evidence of all circumstances existing at the time of the exchange of promises or time of the offer and acceptance. You should not consider any different, but unexpressed meanings intended by the parties.

5. Fraud and Deceit—Fraudulent Misrepresentation—Issues Made by the Pleadings—Fraud—Defendant (Optional)

The plaintiff claims that the defendant made the following statements:

> You know me, I'll transfer to you the stock I promised. You know it has good value. It is some of my best holdings.

The plaintiff claims that the statements were false statements of material facts.

The plaintiff further claims that the defendant knew the statements were false or believed the statements to be false or made the statements in reckless disregard of whether they were true or false.

The plaintiff further claims that the defendant made the statements with the intent to induce the plaintiff to not sue him for his past breach of his promise to reimburse him for his travel expenses.

The plaintiff further claims that he reasonably believed the statements and did not sue in justifiable reliance on the truth of the statements.

The plaintiff further claims that he sustained damages as the result of his reliance.

The defendant denies that he made false statements of facts. He denies that any of the claimed statements were material. He denies that he knew or believed the claimed statements to be false and denies that any claimed statements were made in reckless disregard of the statements' truth or falsity. The defendant also denies that he intended to induce the plaintiff to act in any way; the defendant claims he did not know the plaintiff was contemplating suing him and denies that the plaintiff reasonably believed the listed stock had any value, in justifiable reliance on the truth of the statements. He denies that damage resulted to the plaintiff from his reliance.

6. Materiality

A statement is material when a reasonable prospective purchaser might consider the fact or omission important. The question is whether a reasonable person would attach importance to the misinterpreted or omitted fact in determining his or her course of action. Facts are material if they are facts that, in reasonable and objective contemplation, might affect the value of the securities being offered. An omitted fact is material if there is a substantial likelihood that a reasonable shareholder would consider it important in deciding whether to purchase the stock.

For a fact to be material, there must be a substantial likelihood that the disclosure of the omitted fact would have been viewed by the reasonable investor as having significantly altered the "total mix" of information made available.

7. Fraud and Deceit—Burden of Proof on the Issues—Alternative One—Fraudulent Misrepresentation—One Plaintiff and One Defendant—Clear and Convincing Evidence Only as to Certain Elements (Optional)

The plaintiff has the burden of proving each of the following propositions by clear and convincing evidence:

1. The defendant made false statements of material facts;
2. The defendant (knew) (or) (believed) the statements were false, or the defendant made the statements in reckless disregard of whether they were true or false.

The plaintiff has the burden of proving that each of the following propositions is more probably true than not true:

3. The defendant made the statements with the intent to induce the plaintiff to forgo making further demands for reimbursement of his travel expenses;
4. The plaintiff reasonably believed the statements and left the employment of the defendants in justifiable reliance on the truth of the statements;
5. The plaintiff's damages resulted from his reliance.

If you find from your consideration of all the evidence that propositions one and two have been proved by clear and convincing evidence and that propositions three, four, and five are more probably true than not true, then your verdict should be for the plaintiff.

On the other hand, if you find from your consideration of all the evidence that any of these propositions has not been proved as required in this instruction, then your verdict should be for the defendant.

8. Damages—Yount's Damages

If you find that it was a term of the severance agreement that Harold Molitor and/or MMG would transfer the stock listed in the severance agreement to Stephen Yount within the terms set forth in the agreement and extension, then Stephen Yount is entitled to recover the value of those stock at the time the transfer was supposed to have occurred.

9. Punitive Damages—Willful and Wanton Conduct (Optional)

In addition to compensatory damages, the law permits you under certain circumstances to award punitive damages. If you find that Harold Molitor's conduct was fraudulent, willful, and wanton, and proximately caused damages to the plaintiff, and if you believe that justice and the public good require it, you may award an amount of money that will punish Harold Molitor and discourage him and others from similar conduct. In arriving at your decision as to the amount of punitive damages, you should consider the following three questions. The first question is the most important to determine the amount of punitive damages:

1. How reprehensible was the defendant's conduct? On this subject, you should consider the following:
    a) The facts and circumstances of the defendant's conduct;
    b) The [financial] vulnerability of the plaintiff;
    c) The duration of the misconduct;

- d) The frequency of defendant's misconduct;
- e) Whether the harm was physical as opposed to economic;
- f) Whether defendant tried to conceal the misconduct.

2. What actual and potential harm did the defendant's conduct cause to the plaintiff in this case?
3. What amount of money is necessary to punish the defendant and discourage the defendant and others from future wrongful conduct in light of the defendant's financial condition?

The amount of punitive damages must be reasonable and in proportion to the actual and potential harm suffered by the plaintiff.

Nita Instruction 4:01—Concluding Instruction

The Court did not in any way, and does not, by these instructions, give or intimate any opinions as to what has or has not been proven in the case, or as to what are or are not the facts of the case. No one of these instructions states all of the law applicable, but all of them must be taken, read, and considered together as they are connected to each other as a whole. You must not be concerned with the wisdom of any rule of law. Regardless of any opinions you may have as to what the law ought to be, it would be a violation of your sworn duty to base a verdict on any other view of the law than that given in the instructions of the court.

STATE OF NITA

CENTRAL, ss. **SUPERIOR COURT**

CIVIL ACTION NO.

STEPHEN F. YOUNT, **Plaintiff**	)	
v.	)	Jury Verdict (Contract Only)
MOLITOR MANAGEMENT GROUP, INC., **and HAROLD A. MOLITOR** **Defendants**	)	

YOU ARE TO SIGN AND RETURN ONLY ONE VERDICT.

I. SPECIAL VERDICT FORM #1

We, the Jury, and each of us finds:

1. For the Plaintiff in the amount of $_________________
2. For the defendant ___________________________

[YOU MAY ANSWER EITHER QUESTION 1 OR 2 BUT NOT BOTH.]

____

Date Foreperson

STATE OF NITA

CENTRAL, ss. **SUPERIOR COURT**

CIVIL ACTION NO.

STEPHEN F. YOUNT, **Plaintiff**	)	
v.	)	Jury Verdict (Contract Only)
MOLITOR MANAGEMENT GROUP, INC., and HAROLD A. MOLITOR **Defendants**	)	

YOU ARE TO SIGN AND RETURN ONLY ONE VERDICT.

I. SPECIAL VERDICT FORM #2

Did Stephen F. Yount prove a severance agreement existed between him and Harold Molitor and or the Molitor Management Group, MMG for the exchange of stock listed as part of the severance agreement, and that agreement was extended on October 4, till the end of January 31, YR-3?

Yes _____ No _____

If your answer is no, this concludes your deliberations.

Did Stephen F. Yount prove that the severance agreement required Harold Molitor and or MMG to transfer to Stephen F. Yount stocks listed in the severance agreement and that neither Harold Molitor nor MMG transferred such stock during the time of the agreement?

Yes _____ No _____

If your answer is no, this concludes your deliberations.

What amount of damages (including interest, if any) has Stephen F. Yount proven? Enter the amount in dollars: $________________

If your answer on each of the questions is a unanimous yes, have the foreperson sign the verdict form.

____

Foreperson

Impeachment Problems

Problem 1

Yount testifies on direct examination as follows: "I remembered I was relieved having taken the photo of him signing, knowing that Susan was insisting on seeing a signed agreement. And I'm sure that I sent it to her as I was leaving his office."

Yount Deposition, Page 20, Line 17

Q. When did you send her this photo of Molitor's signature?

A. Well, I don't remember exactly. I have a vague memory she was demanding to see the signed copy. I wasn't exactly sure how to send it to her at the time. It was a new phone and I was still getting used to . . . learning how to send photos. I might not have sent it until the next day.

Problem 2

Harold Molitor testifies at trial as follows: Q: "What was your reaction to his request to sign an agreement?" A: "I was furious. I refused to sign. Even when he insisted I continued to refuse to sign. I don't know how he would have come away with the impression that I had agreed to the extended agreement."

Molitor Deposition, Page 28, Line 39

Q. Did you ever say or do anything to give the impression you were extending the agreement?

A: At one point, I may have made of show of air-signing my name across a piece of paper. I don't remember if it was on the agreement itself or otherwise. It probably was.